"To lead like Christ is to bleed while you lead — to love, serve, and sacrifice even when it hurts."

— Winston Peccoo

BLEEDING WHILE LEADING:

THE SILENT PAIN BEHIND PUBLIC STRENGTH

Winston Peccoo

BLEEDING WHILE LEADING: THE SILENT PAIN BEHIND PUBLIC STRENGTH

Copyright ©2025 Winston Peccoo

Published by:

ISBN: 978-1-0696329-2-0

All rights reserved. Total or partial reproduction of this work, (text, illustrations, diagrams), information processing and transmission, be it by electronic or mechanical means, by photocopying or by any other medium without permission in writing from the publisher is prohibited and punishable by law.

Contact Reason Publishers at reasonwithrobdon@gmail.com
Cover design by: Robdon Designs

TABLE OF CONTENTS

INTRODUCTION —————————————————— 7
CHAPTER 1 ——————————————————— 11
  The Cost of the Call ——————————————— 11
CHAPTER 2 ——————————————————— 20
  Silent Tears, Public Applause ————————— 20
CHAPTER 3 ——————————————————— 50
  The Loneliness of the Mantle ———————— 50
CHAPTER 4 ——————————————————— 113
  Emotional Bleeding ————————————— 113
CHAPTER 5 ——————————————————— 127
  Spiritual Bleeding —————————————— 127
CHAPTER 6 ——————————————————— 137
  Mental Bleeding ——————————————— 137
CHAPTER 7 ——————————————————— 146
  Physical Bleeding —————————————— 146
CHAPTER 8 ——————————————————— 152
  The Mask of Strength ———————————— 152
CHAPTER 9 ——————————————————— 162
  When Weakness is a Taboo ————————— 162

CHAPTER 10 — **171**

Leading While Limping — 171

CHAPTER 11 — **179**

Healing is a Journey, not a Moment

179

CHAPTER 12 — **182**

The Ultimate Bleeding Leader — 182

CHAPTER 13 — **191**

Safe Spaces and Safe People

191

CHAPTER 14 — **198**

Boundaries and Balance — 198

CHAPTER 15 — **206**

Leading with Scars, Not Open Wounds — 206

CHAPTER 16 — **212**

Beauty from Bleeding — 212

APPENDICES — **219**

INTRODUCTION
The Paradox of Leadership Pain

Leadership is often seen as a position of strength, confidence, and clarity. Leaders are expected to have the answers, remain composed under pressure, and motivate others to move forward, even in uncertain terrain. But beneath the surface of this noble calling lies a sobering truth: **leaders often hurt in silence**. The very ones who are called to lift others are frequently carrying wounds of their own—wounds they dare not reveal.

This is the paradox of leadership pain: while leading others toward growth, progress, or healing, leaders themselves are often bleeding. They are expected to be resilient, yet they are human. They are expected to inspire, yet sometimes they are discouraged. They are expected to have vision, yet there are nights when they cannot see their way clearly.

The Myth of Invincibility
There is a widely held but deeply damaging myth that leaders must be invincible. Society glorifies strength and success but often leaves no room for struggle. We assume that if someone is at the top, they must be fine. If they are preaching, teaching, managing, or guiding others, surely, they must have it all together. This myth isolates leaders, causing them to suppress their vulnerabilities, mask their emotional bruises, and suffer quietly rather than seek help or admit weakness.

This expectation can become a prison. The pressure to always be strong causes leaders to ignore their own needs, delay their healing, and carry burdens that no one else sees. And because many fear being perceived as weak or inadequate, they choose silence over honesty—even when that silence is suffocating.

Why This Book Matters
This book is written for *every leader who has ever cried in secret*, for every aspiring leader who must understand the weight that leadership carries, and for every follower who wants to better support those at the helm. It is not just a leadership manual; it is a mirror held up to the souls of those who carry the responsibility of others.

Leadership is not just about platforms, strategies, or influence. It's also about the cost. It's about the emotional, mental, and spiritual toll it takes to stand in front of others while sometimes falling apart behind the scenes. It's about recognizing that leadership pain does not disqualify a person—it deepens them. When acknowledged and processed, it becomes a well of wisdom, empathy, and authenticity.

A Personal Reflection
I remember the Sunday morning I stood before my congregation to preach hope and healing, just hours after learning that a close family member had passed away. I smiled. I prayed. I led. But inside, I was broken. That day, I realized that ministry and leadership do not pause for personal grief. It was one of many moments that taught me how painful leadership can be—and how necessary it is to create spaces for honest conversations about that pain.

A Scriptural Perspective
No one embodies the paradox of leadership pain more than Jesus Christ. Hanging on the cross, bruised, bleeding, and mocked, He was still fulfilling His leadership assignment—redeeming humanity. He was in agony, yet He forgave. He was pierced, yet He led a thief into paradise. He was abandoned, yet He entrusted His mother to the care of another. Even in suffering, Jesus modeled sacrificial leadership.

His pain was not a sign of failure; it was the price of purpose. Likewise, modern-day leaders must understand that pain is often a companion on the path of purpose. When we look to Jesus, we see that leadership pain is not the end of the story—it is part of the process of redemption and transformation.

This book is a call to honesty, healing, and hope. It seeks to affirm that leadership pain is real, but so is the grace that sustains. As we journey through its pages, may every leader find permission to feel, courage to face their wounds, and strength to keep leading—wiser, deeper, and more whole.

PART ONE: THE WOUNDS OF LEADERSHIP

CHAPTER 1
The Cost of the Call

There is a hidden weight that every true leader must bear. It cannot be measured by public applause, titles, or influence. It is the *unseen cost*—the part of the calling no one tells you about. Before the platform, before the recognition, there is the pain, the private breaking, and the refining fire of obedience.

The Unseen Weight Leaders Carry
Many admire leaders from a distance—drawn to their confidence, captivated by their eloquence, and inspired by their strength. They seem to walk with grace, speak with clarity, and carry a certain authority that commands attention. But what most do not see is the silent weight they bear—the pressures, the prayers, the personal battles that accompany the mantle of leadership.

Leadership, particularly spiritual leadership, is not a glamorous position—it is a sacrificial calling. It often demands more than it gives. It stretches a person to the edges of their endurance and requires a depth of faith that is tested continually in private. The applause of people rarely reflects the anguish of the leader's soul. Behind every powerful sermon, strategy, or decision is often a sleepless night, a broken heart, or a hidden tear.

Leaders are called to carry the burdens of others even while wrestling with their own. They must remain strong when others collapse, offer clarity when confusion abounds, and serve as anchors in storms they never asked for. They are expected to have answers, even when God is silent. They pour into others even when their cup feels empty. They are physicians bleeding while treating others. Warriors wounded, yet still expected to fight.

They are called to lead while bleeding—navigating betrayal, rejection, and criticism with grace. They must pray while in pain, interceding for others' breakthroughs while waiting on their own. They smile in the spotlight, masking the exhaustion and emotional toll that leadership quietly extracts. What the public praises, the private self often questions. And yet, they endure.

The leader's tears often fall in places no one sees—at the altar, in their car, behind closed doors, in the dead of night. They grieve in silence because their pain must not become a stumbling block for those they lead. Their vulnerability is limited not by pride, but by responsibility. Not all wounds can be voiced. Not all battles can be shared.

To be called is to be burdened. Not because God delights in seeing His servants suffer, but because the weight of the call demands a matching weight of character. And character is not built in comfort. It is forged in the fire of affliction, in the wilderness seasons, in the hidden places where no applause exists—only God's refining presence.

The oil that flows from a leader's life is costly. It does not come cheaply. It comes from being crushed, pressed, and processed. The authority they carry is the fruit of tears, tests, and tenacity. Their ability to lead flows not from perfection but from brokenness submitted to God.

So, the next time you see a leader stand tall, remember: their posture is not a reflection of ease, but of endurance. Pray for them. Encourage them. Cover them. Because while they may carry others with strength, they, too, need someone to carry them in prayer. They may be shepherds, but even shepherds need rest, need grace, need healing.

True leadership is not about being exalted. It is about being emptied for a cause greater than self. It is the sacred tension between calling and crushing. And yet, by the grace of God, they carry on—not because they are superhuman, but because they are super-dependent on the One who called them.

Biblical Leaders Who Bled
Throughout Scripture, we are presented not with sanitized success stories, but with raw and honest journeys of men who bled—physically, emotionally, and spiritually—because of the divine call on their lives. Their stories shatter the illusion that divine calling is glamorous or easy. God's calling is glorious, yes—but it is also grievous. It demands everything. To lead in God's kingdom is to carry a cross. It is to bleed before you ever wear a crown.

David: The Anointed Fugitive
David's story is often romanticized—the shepherd boy who slew Goliath and became Israel's greatest king. But between the anointing and the enthronement came years of unimaginable suffering. Though chosen by God, David was hunted like a criminal by Saul. He hid in caves, feigned madness, and wandered in enemy territories. The betrayal by trusted allies like Doeg the

Edomite and even his son Absalom left scars deeper than any sword could inflict.

His pain is woven into the Psalms: "I am worn out from my groaning. All night long I flood my bed with weeping" (Psalm 6:6). His leadership came with isolation, internal torment, and moments of despair. Yet in all his bleeding, David pressed into God. His wounds did not disqualify him—they prepared him. His brokenness became the channel through which God's heart could be revealed to Israel.

Moses: The Burdened Mediator
Moses' journey began in privilege but transitioned to obscurity. After fleeing Egypt, he spent forty years tending sheep in Midian—a far cry from the royal courts of Pharaoh. When God called him at the burning bush, Moses did not jump with enthusiasm. He questioned, doubted, and resisted. Why? Because he knew the cost. Leadership wasn't a title; it was a burden.

And indeed, Moses carried the weight of a stiff-necked people who murmured and rebelled at every turn. He often stood between them and God's wrath, interceding, pleading, and even offering himself in their place (Exodus 32:32). He led them through the wildernesses—not just geographically, but spiritually. And yet, he would not enter the Promised Land. Leadership, for Moses, meant obedience without reward, sacrifice without applause.

Paul: The Suffering Servant
No New Testament leader bore more visible scars than Paul. His resume was littered with pain: flogging, imprisonment, shipwreck, hunger, rejection, and eventually martyrdom. Yet

Paul never portrayed suffering as a curse. Instead, he saw it as confirmation of his calling. "For it has been granted to you on behalf of Christ not only to believe in him, but also to suffer for him" (Philippians 1:29).

Paul's bleeding was not in vain—it birthed churches, letters, and a legacy of faith that endures to this day. His chains advanced the gospel. His wounds preached louder than his words. He knew that to carry the gospel was to carry the cross, and he did so willingly, declaring, "I consider everything a loss because of the surpassing worth of knowing Christ Jesus my Lord" (Philippians 3:8).

Jesus: The Crucified King
At the center of all biblical leadership stands Jesus, the Son of God, who bled not just for a mission, but for humanity. From the manger to the cross, His life was marked by rejection, misunderstanding, and suffering. Isaiah described Him as "despised and rejected by men, a man of sorrows, and familiar with suffering" (Isaiah 53:3).

His leadership was not enforced by power but embodied in love. He washed feet, wept at tombs, and ultimately laid down His life for those who hated Him. The cross was not a detour in His calling—it was the destination. He bled, not just as a sacrifice, but as a model for all who would follow. "Whoever wants to be my disciple must deny themselves and take up their cross daily and follow me" (Luke 9:23).

The Cost of the Call

Leadership in God's kingdom is not a casual invitation—it is a summons that demands everything. It will cost you more than you ever imagined. It will break your pride, stretch your faith, test your endurance, and expose your deepest fears and insecurities. The call is not convenient; it is costly. It does not stroke the ego; it crucifies it.

To be chosen by God is both an honor and a burden. It is the invitation to walk a path where applause is rare and opposition is guaranteed. The call will isolate you, confuse you, humble you, and sometimes even crush you. But in all of this, it will also *refine you*. It will strip away the superficial and anchor you in what is eternal. It will deepen your dependence on God, shape your character in the furnace of affliction, and mold you into a vessel through which His glory can shine undiluted.

To be called is to bleed.

It is to step into spiritual warfare, internal struggle, and relational misunderstandings. It is to weep in secret while leading in public. It is to carry burdens no one sees and fight battles no one applauds. It is to be misunderstood, misrepresented, and sometimes even mistreated—all for the sake of the One who bled for you first.

But to bleed in your calling is not a sign of failure; it is evidence that you have been counted *worthy* to share in Christ's sufferings *and* His glory (Romans 8:17). Wounds sustained in obedience are not signs of weakness—they are marks of loyalty. They are sacred scars that heaven honors.

If you find yourself weary, wounded, or wondering why your calling feels so painful, know this: **you are not abandoned—you are being shaped.** God is not punishing you; He is preparing you. Every scar has a purpose. Every tear is noticed. Every season of hidden pain builds an unseen strength.

He does not call the bloodless. He calls the *broken*. He calls the *brave*. He calls the ones willing to bleed, because through their bleeding, He brings healing. First to them. Then through them, to the world.

Moses bled in the wilderness. David bled in caves and on battlefields. Jeremiah wept in the dungeons. Paul bore scars from beatings, rejection, and shipwrecks. Even Jesus, the perfect Son, was called to lead by dying first. What makes us think we will lead without cost?

So, if you're bleeding in your calling, rejoice—not because the pain is pleasant, but because the pain is *purposeful*. God is writing something eternal with your obedience. Stay the course. Lean in. Keep walking.

Your scars are sacred. Your tears are not wasted. And your calling is still sure.

Obedience Doesn't Remove Suffering
One of the most dangerous misconceptions in modern Christianity is the belief that obeying God guarantees a life free from hardship. This distorted gospel suggests that following Christ is a path to comfort, ease, and unbroken success. But Scripture—and the life of Christ Himself—tell a different story. The truth is sobering yet liberating: **obedience to God does not**

remove suffering; in many cases, it invites it.

When we examine the lives of the faithful throughout the Bible, we don't see a trail of uninterrupted blessings or worldly applause. Instead, we find stories marked by pain, persecution, and trials. Abraham obeyed and left his homeland—only to wander as a foreigner. Joseph followed God's hand into Egypt, but through betrayal and imprisonment. David was anointed king, yet spent years fleeing for his life. The prophets obeyed, and they were mocked, rejected, and martyred.

And at the center of it all stands Jesus—the very embodiment of obedience. He was "obedient to the point of death—even death on a cross" (Philippians 2:8). He didn't suffer because He disobeyed. He suffered *because* He obeyed.

Jesus never said, "Follow Me and life will be easy." He said, **"If anyone would come after Me, let him deny himself, take up his cross daily, and follow Me"** (Luke 9:23). That call isn't metaphorical, it's radical. The cross is not a symbol of convenience or casual faith. It is an instrument of death. To follow Christ means to die daily to self, comfort, pride, and personal agenda. It is a surrender so deep that it may cost you everything: your comfort, your career, your ambitions, and sometimes even your relationships.

But in that dying, something holy is birthed. In the furnace of suffering, our faith is refined. In the breaking, we are made whole. In the stripping away of worldly security, we encounter the unshakable sufficiency of Christ. Obedience strips us of the illusion that we are in control and brings us face to face with our desperate need for God.

Suffering does not mean God has abandoned you. It often means He is nearer than ever. **In the fire, we discover the God who still speaks. In the storm, we learn to hear His whisper.** And in the wilderness, we are reminded that His presence is our greatest reward.

Obedience may not always bring immediate reward, but it always brings eternal significance. God uses our trials to conform us to the image of Christ, not to destroy us but to refine us. "For our light and momentary troubles are achieving for us an eternal glory that far outweighs them all" (2 Corinthians 4:17).

So don't buy into the lie that your suffering is evidence of failure. If you're walking in obedience and still facing hardship, you're in good company. The road of obedience is narrow and often costly, but it leads to deeper intimacy with God. The applause of men may fade, but the affirmation of Heaven endures forever.

Let obedience be your offering, not because it guarantees ease, but because it aligns you with the heart of the One who suffered for you. There is power in obedience. Not the kind that avoids the fire, but the kind that walks through it and comes out transformed.

Reflection Questions:
1. Am I willing to accept the hidden cost of the call, not just the visible reward?
2. How do I respond when obedience leads me into difficult, lonely, or painful places?
3. Which biblical leader's journey resonates most with my current season, and what can I learn from their pain?
4.

CHAPTER 2
Silent Tears, Public Applause

There is a haunting paradox that many people, especially those in leadership, ministry, performance, or high-visibility roles—know all too well: being admired publicly while suffering silently. It is possible to be celebrated on stages, applauded in crowds, and respected in rooms—yet still cry yourself to sleep behind closed doors. This chapter explores the deep emotional disconnect between public praise and private pain, the emotional toll of performing while broken, and the hidden cost of being everyone's hero but your own.

The Disconnect Between Public Praise and Private Pain
It is a lonely and exhausting existence to be celebrated publicly while suffering silently in private. There's a deep ache that comes with being admired by many but intimately known by none. When others look at you, they see competence, charisma, and confidence. They see the carefully curated highlights—your resilience in chaos, your grace under pressure, your polished words and poised demeanor. They assume all is well because you've mastered the art of looking whole.

But inside, there's a war no one hears. Your heart bleeds quietly behind the scenes, tucked away beneath layers of composure. You smile not because you're always joyful, but because you've learned that being visibly broken makes people uncomfortable. So, you put on the smile, deliver the words, lift others' burdens, and play your role. You are the strong one, the reliable one, the anchor when others are drifting. And yet, who anchors you?

When the crowds disperse, when the messages stop, and the noise dies down, you're left alone with the weight of what no one sees. The applause that once energized you now echoes hollow in the silence of your solitude. You wonder: **Does anyone see the person behind the platform? Behind the pulpit? Behind the parental role? Behind the professionalism?** You're not looking for pity—you're yearning for presence. For someone to hold space with you, not because you're strong, but because sometimes, you're not.

The truth is, you're not being fake, you're being functional. There's a difference. You've become highly skilled at managing the tension between public responsibility and private vulnerability. You've learned how to keep going, to lead in pain, to show up even when everything inside you wants to shut down. Not because you're inauthentic, but because people depend on you. You're a leader, a counselor, a parent, a mentor, a minister—so you suppress the tremble in your voice and keep walking, even when your knees buckle in secret.

But that suppression takes a toll.

The danger is that in being everything for everyone, you lose permission to be anything but strong. You become imprisoned by the very image people love you for. Vulnerability becomes a luxury you no longer feel entitled to. You start to believe that being seen as weak will cost you your platform, your influence, or worse—people's respect. And so you suffer silently. Cry in the shower. Pray on your pillow. Bleed behind closed doors.

But even the strongest among us need safe places. You need sacred spaces where performance ends and presence begins. Where you don't have to explain yourself, impress anyone, or hold it together. Where you can be *seen*, not for what you do, but for who you are. Where your tears don't confuse people, and your silence isn't judged. Where someone can say, *"You don't have to be strong here. You can just be."*

If this resonates with you, hear this truth: **Your pain is valid, even if it's invisible. Your humanity matters, even if you're the one people lean on. You deserve to be known, not just admired. And it's okay to need help, even when you're the helper.**

You are not weak for wanting to be seen. You are not failing for feeling tired. You are not broken beyond repair.

You are a soul deserving of care—not because of your role, but because you are human.

And while people may celebrate the public version of you, may you have the courage to let at least a few into the private version too—the version that aches, questions, doubts, and bleeds. Because healing doesn't happen in hiding. Healing happens in being known.

When You're Celebrated but Empty
There's a quiet agony that creeps in when the applause grows louder, but your soul grows quieter. It's the pain of being praised while privately unraveling. You smile for the pictures, respond graciously to the compliments, and keep producing results—but inside, there's a hollow space no amount of applause can reach.

It's a strange place to be: surrounded by admiration yet starved of genuine connection. Loved for what you do, yet unseen for who you are.

Success has a subtle cruelty. It raises you high but often isolates you in the process. The more competent you appear, the fewer people check in on your heart. You become the one everyone looks to for answers, strength, and inspiration, even as your own soul silently bleeds. You perform, preach, lead, counsel, create—functioning with excellence while feeling disconnected from your own essence. You're no longer seen as a person with emotional needs, but as a solution to other people's problems. A platform, not a person. A light to others, while you grope through your own darkness.

The danger of being "highly needed" is that it often disguises the fact that you're deeply neglected. Not by others alone, but sometimes by yourself. You get so used to meeting everyone else's expectations that you stop asking what *you* need. You confuse momentum with meaning, gifting with grounding. But gifting can flow even when your soul is gasping for air. You can still move crowds, still carry out your responsibilities, still impress—until the day you can't. The day the mask cracks, and exhaustion breaks through like a flood.

Worse still, the celebration itself can become a drug. The praise, the claps, the invitations—they feel good in the moment. They affirm that you matter. They whisper that you're worthy. But they never last. When the crowd disperses and the stage is empty, you're left with the silence. And in that silence, the ache returns.

Applause may affirm your work, but it can't anchor your soul. Recognition may fuel your ego, but it cannot restore your spirit.

There's a particular loneliness that comes from being everyone's inspiration while having no one safe enough to fall apart with. No room to grieve. No space to say, "I'm not okay." And so, you keep pushing. Keep showing up. Keep performing. Hoping maybe the next round of affirmation will finally reach that wounded part of you. But it never does—because no external celebration can heal an internal emptiness.

So, what do you do when you're celebrated but empty?

You pause. You turn down the noise. You allow yourself to be human again. You let God, not performance, define your worth. You pursue authenticity over applause, rest over hustle, intimacy over image. You stop finding your value in what you produce and start rediscovering it in who you are. In who you are when no one's watching. In who you are when you're not "needed," not "on," not "doing."

You find spaces where you can be known, not just noticed. Where your tears are not a weakness, but a language. Where your silence is not judged, but understood. You lean into healing. You seek the kind of community that doesn't require a title, a gift, or a performance—just *you*. Broken. Becoming. Beloved.

Because you were never meant to live off applause. You were meant to live out of fullness.

Performing While Broken
One of the most heartbreaking and painful realities that many people face, particularly those in leadership or caregiving roles, is the constant need to perform while grappling with internal wounds, brokenness, or unhealed struggles. Whether it's a worship leader whose heart is shattered yet still praises, a preacher delivering sermons of hope while secretly feeling hopeless, a counselor offering wise guidance while struggling with their own emotional battles, or a parent or spouse holding a family together while feeling fragmented inside—this experience of "performing while broken" is far too common.

It's an emotional paradox, this delicate balance between purpose and pain. You go through the motions of life, fulfilling responsibilities and obligations, but deep down, you feel as though you are falling apart. The internal bleeding continues, but outwardly, you appear whole. It's the constant juxtaposition of nurturing others while needing healing yourself.

The Cost of Internal Struggles
The weight of silent suffering is not just heavy, it is crushing. It lingers quietly beneath smiles, sermons, encouragements, and comforting words. Those whom others lean on for strength—leaders, mentors, parents, caregivers, pastors, friends—often find themselves shouldering storms of their own with no one to turn to, and no time or space to fall apart. They become professionals at hiding their own pain behind the noble pursuit of serving others.

You might be one of them. You speak life and hope into the hearts of the broken. You offer your presence to the lonely, your strength to the weary, and your prayers to the desperate. But beneath it all, you're unraveling. You're standing in the middle of a storm, soaked to the skin, holding up an umbrella for everyone but yourself. The rain pelts down, yet you keep smiling, keep helping, keep giving—while your own soul cries out for rest.

You offer peace, even when your own heart is a battlefield. You pour out comfort while quietly aching inside. You inspire faith while wrestling with doubt. You lead others into healing while carrying wounds of your own that never had the chance to scab over, let alone heal. You may be running on empty, emotionally drained and spiritually depleted from giving more than you have. And still, you keep showing up.

This doesn't make you a hypocrite. It makes you human. It makes you someone who has chosen to walk in purpose, even when your path is riddled with pain. It reveals the complexity of a calling that demands both strength and sacrifice, both vulnerability and valor. You are living proof that being called does not mean being invincible.

But even purpose has its price when it is not balanced with care for your own soul. Left unchecked, this internal tension can grow into resentment, disillusionment, spiritual dryness, emotional fatigue, and even physical sickness. The body begins to echo what the heart has been silently screaming for years—"I can't carry all of this alone."

The danger is not in the struggle itself—struggle is a part of life and growth. The danger lies in staying silent about it. In pretending that you're fine when you're not. In being there for everyone else but refusing to be honest about your own need for support, love, prayer, and rest.

You were never meant to carry it all alone. Even Jesus, when He carried the cross, stumbled under its weight—and Simon of Cyrene was summoned to help Him carry it the rest of the way. If the Son of God needed help on His hardest day, what makes you think you don't?

Let this be a reminder: it's okay to be needed and still need others. It's okay to lead and still cry. To serve and still rest. To pour out and still retreat to be refilled. To be strong and still have moments of weakness.

Healing begins when we stop hiding. Restoration begins when we start receiving the same grace we freely give to others. Let go of the guilt that tells you you must always be the strong one. Let go of the shame that says your brokenness disqualifies your calling. It doesn't.

You are allowed to rest. You are allowed to feel. You are allowed to heal. And you are allowed to be human.

The Hidden Dangers of Ignoring the Brokenness
There is a silent danger in pressing forward without ever tending to your wounds. At first, it feels noble—selfless, even. You're the dependable one, the strong one, the helper. You carry others. You perform. You achieve. You meet expectations. But underneath it all, something begins to crack.

As time goes on, the consequences of neglecting your own brokenness begin to seep into every corner of your life. The more you give, the more you feel yourself running dry. You pour out encouragement, support, energy, and time—but rarely do you pause long enough to acknowledge your own fatigue, your own sadness, your own need to be seen. Eventually, you begin to operate on empty, trying to offer from a place that has not been filled in a long time.

When your pain is never validated, and your struggles are quietly shoved aside, you begin to internalize a dangerous message: that your value is contingent upon your performance. That you matter *because* of what you do, not *who* you are. You start to wear productivity and responsibility like armor, believing that if you ever stop, everything might fall apart—including you.

In this performance-based identity, the concept of being "enough" without output becomes a foreign language. Rest feels like laziness. Asking for help feels like weakness. Vulnerability feels like failure. You convince yourself that if you don't keep showing up perfectly, you'll be overlooked, unloved, or replaced. So, you hustle harder, smile wider, and suppress deeper. But this isn't strength—it's survival.

Over time, this mindset steals from you. It disconnects you from your true self—the part of you that was created not just to do, but to be. To be whole. To be known. To be loved, even when you have nothing left to offer. Without healing, performance becomes an addiction. You chase the next achievement, the next "thank you," the next applause, hoping it will silence the ache inside. But it never truly satisfies. It only feeds the illusion.

And here's the deeper danger: the longer you live this way, the more your identity fuses with your image. You forget who you were before the expectations, before the roles, before the masks.

Your heart longs for rest, for authenticity, for a space where you can simply *be*—imperfect, in-process, and still worthy.

Healing is not weakness; it is wisdom. It's choosing to confront the pain you've buried so you can finally live whole, not fractured. It's reclaiming the truth that you are valuable, not for what you produce, but because you exist. Because you are human. Because you are loved by God.

The path to freedom begins with one brave choice: to stop ignoring the brokenness and start facing it with grace. To ask for help. To rest without guilt. To stop performing and start healing. You don't need to earn your worth—it was never up for negotiation.

You are enough, even when you're not doing. You are seen, even when you're quiet. You are loved, even when you're healing. And the most powerful gift you can give others isn't your perfection—it's your wholeness.

The Burnout Epidemic
There is a silent epidemic sweeping through our society—one that rarely makes headlines but leaves countless individuals emotionally drained, spiritually empty, and physically exhausted. It's the **burnout epidemic**, and at the heart of it lies an unaddressed brokenness that many carry in silence.

This burnout isn't just about overwork or poor time management. It's deeper than that. It is rooted in the **unrelenting pressure to appear strong**, especially among those in leadership positions. Leaders—whether in the workplace, church, family, or community—are often placed on pedestals, expected to be steady, composed, and immune to the emotional turbulence that others experience. They're the ones others run to, the ones who "always have the answer," who seem to never need help themselves. But behind the calm exterior, many are barely holding on.

These leaders carry **silent burdens**—grief, personal doubts, marital struggles, fatigue, trauma, and spiritual dryness—that are hidden behind forced smiles and polished presentations. Few ever stop to ask them, "How are you—*really?*" And even fewer create safe spaces where they are allowed to be **weak, tired, or broken** without judgment or consequence. The result? They continue to pour out while running on empty, giving from reserves they no longer have, until they collapse inwardly.

And this isn't limited to CEOs or pastors. The burnout epidemic extends to **mothers, fathers, caregivers, teachers, mentors**, and anyone who continually gives of themselves for the benefit of others. These are the people who rise early and sleep late, who counsel others while no one notices their own tears, who give and give, often without pause, recognition, or replenishment.

In today's image-driven culture, **the pressure to maintain an illusion of invulnerability** can be suffocating. We reward strength, independence, and hustle, but we shame rest, vulnerability, and honest admission of need. Those who try to keep up this unsustainable façade end up **emotionally depleted**, spiritually dry, physically worn out, and sometimes even **numb to life** itself.

Over time, this constant internal strain leads to:
- **Chronic fatigue** that rests doesn't solve.
- **Resentment** toward the people they serve.

- **Loss of purpose**, questioning their calling or value.
- **Mental health struggles**, such as anxiety and depression.
- **Identity crisis**, where they no longer know who they are apart from what they do.

The Real Danger: Burnout in Silence

The most dangerous form of burnout is the one that happens **in silence**—unnoticed by others and even unacknowledged by the individual. It festers beneath the surface until it explodes in the form of moral failure, broken relationships, complete withdrawal, or a total breakdown.

This is why **healing must become a priority, not a luxury**. Leaders, givers, and caregivers must learn that **being human is not a weakness** and vulnerability is not failure. True strength is found in **recognizing your limits**, not in denying them.

The Way Forward

To combat the burnout epidemic, we must create cultures—at work, at home, in faith communities—where **rest is valued, emotional honesty is welcomed**, and **asking for help is a sign** of wisdom, not weakness. Moving forward we must:

- **Check in on the strong ones.** Ask them how they are *really* doing and give them space to answer without pressure or expectation.
- **Encourage rhythms of rest and restoration.** That may look like sabbaticals, therapy, spiritual retreats, or simply learning to say "no."
- **Model vulnerability.** When leaders and parents admit their own struggles, it permits others to do the same.

- **Build support systems.** No one was meant to carry life's burdens alone. Healthy friendships, mentorship, and accountability are vital.
- **Redefine success.** Instead of equating success with non-stop productivity, we must begin to honor wholeness, peace, and inner health.

Burnout is not just a personal issue—it's a **communal concern**. If we don't learn to care for our caregivers and support our leaders, we'll continue to see emotional collapse behind polished performance. Let's normalize healing. Let's dignify rest. Let's embrace humanity. And let's begin asking the brave question—*"How are you, really?"*

The Importance of Healing and Restoration
Healing is not a luxury; it is a fundamental requirement for a meaningful, purpose-driven life. Without healing, we live fractured lives, offering only fragments of ourselves to others. We may mask our pain behind accomplishments, titles, or busyness, but unresolved wounds will always find a way to surface. Healing, therefore, is not just about moving past pain; it's about becoming whole so that we can love, lead, serve, and relate from a place of authenticity and inner strength.

True healing begins with honesty. It demands that we stop pretending we're fine and confront the parts of our story that still sting. It invites us to sit with our discomfort, trace our pain to its root, and admit where we are still bleeding. Healing is not weakness—it is courage. It's a brave decision to pause, reflect, and engage in the hard work of restoration rather than pushing forward while internally deteriorating.

We must understand that asking for help is not an admission of failure but a declaration of strength. There is no shame in admitting that you're tired, wounded, or overwhelmed. Your worth is not tied to your level of perfection, productivity, or emotional invincibility. You are still valuable—even when you're broken, even when you're not okay. Healing does not diminish who you are; it reclaims the parts of you that pain tried to steal.

This truth is especially critical for leaders. Often, those who lead others feel the pressure to maintain an image of constant strength. They carry the burdens of many but rarely feel permission to acknowledge their own. But leadership does not exempt anyone from the human need for healing. In fact, the weight of responsibility makes healing even more urgent.

Healthy leadership flows from a healed life. A leader who ignores their wounds may unconsciously project their pain onto others, make reactive decisions, or lead with insecurity. To lead well, you must first learn how to be led—by wisdom, by God, and by trusted voices who can speak truth and encouragement into your life.

Churches, workplaces, ministries, and families must foster cultures of compassion and restoration, not performance and perfection. We must normalize vulnerability at every level of influence. Leaders need safe spaces where they can take off their armor, confess their weariness, and receive counsel without fear of judgment or disqualification.

Rest is holy. Restoration is essential. And sabbatical seasons should not be seen as indulgent but as integral to long-term effectiveness and emotional sustainability.

Let us not forget: brokenness is not the end of your story. Healing is possible. Restoration is real. But it requires your willingness to slow down, to be honest, and to embrace grace—not only for others but for yourself. When we allow healing to take its full course, we rise stronger, softer, and more equipped to walk in the fullness of who we were created to be.

Restoring Balance
In a world that often measures worth by productivity, it's easy to fall into the trap of believing that our value lies in what we *do* rather than who we *are*. We hustle, we strive, we serve, and we pour out—sometimes to the point of depletion—thinking that more output means greater significance. But the truth is this: **doing does not equate to being.** Our identity is not defined by our performance, our roles, or the applause we receive. It is rooted in our God-given essence—who we are at the core, even when no one is watching.

For those who are givers, helpers, and nurturers, there is a sacred call to pause. You cannot keep pouring from an empty vessel. The most powerful acts of service don't flow from a place of exhaustion, but from a wellspring of inner wholeness and peace. If you've been performing while broken—smiling through pain, giving while grieving, showing up while silently falling apart—it's time to step back and breathe.

Ask yourself:
- What would happen if I stopped performing for a moment?
- What if I permitted myself to stop striving and started healing?
- What if I embraced rest—not as a reward for work done, but as a necessary act of self-compassion and faith?

Rest is not laziness. Rest is not weakness. Rest is restoration. It is the brave acknowledgment that I am not God, and I was never meant to carry everything on my own.

To be nurtured is to lean into the love of God and the support of safe community. It is to remind your soul that *you are enough*, not when you're fixed, but even now—in the midst of your brokenness. Your cracks don't make you useless; they make you human. They make you relatable. They make you real.

Healing doesn't disqualify you from purpose; it prepares you for it.

It transforms your pain into power, your wounds into wisdom, and your weariness into worship. When we allow God to meet us in our lowest, most fragile state, He doesn't turn away. He draws near. And in that nearness, He gently restores, renews, and redefines us—not by what we do, but by whose we are.

So, before you run again, before you say yes again, before you serve again—pause. Let yourself *be*. Let yourself feel. Let yourself heal.

Only from a place of inner healing can we truly become the vessels God intends us to be. Not just active, but *authentic*. Not just busy, but *whole*. Not just performers, but *people*—beloved, enough, and deeply rooted in grace.

In this balance, we find not only our rhythm, but our reason. We rediscover joy. We remember that we were never meant to live in pieces. We were always meant to live in peace.

A Real Story: The Worship Leader Who Broke in Silence

Monica had always been the heart of worship in her church. As one of the most anointed worship leaders in her city, her voice was a unique gift. Every Sunday, as she led the congregation into the presence of God, it was as if the heavens opened. Her melodies brought people to tears, their hearts lifted in ways they couldn't quite explain. She had that rare ability to make people feel connected to the divine, to bring them to a place where worship was no longer just a ritual, but an encounter.

But there was something Monica's congregation never saw. Behind the curtain of applause and reverence, Monica was silently breaking. She had a family — a husband and children — but her home was a place of emotional distance and unspoken pain. Her husband, once her closest confidant, had emotionally checked out. The connection they had shared seemed to have dissolved, leaving a painful void that no amount of ministry could fill. Her children, though still physically present, were drifting away.

On the outside, Monica appeared to have it all together. She was the embodiment of grace and strength. But inside, she was fighting a war. Depression had crept into her heart slowly but surely. She felt overwhelmed, isolated, and desperate, yet she was a master at hiding it. The smile on her face was a mask; the applause she received in church became a substitute for the emotional fulfillment she so desperately needed. Makeup, music, and ministry became her armor, hiding the emptiness she felt within.

"I remember one night," she shared in a quiet, reflective tone, "I had just led an incredibly powerful worship session. The altar was full, people were crying, and miracles were happening. But as soon as I stepped off the stage, I went into the bathroom, locked the door, and cried uncontrollably. I was empty. I had nothing left. I remember whispering to God, 'What about me? Who sings over me?'"

In that moment, Monica realized something profound: she was pouring out to others, but no one was pouring into her. She had given so much of herself in service to God and His people, but she was spiritually and emotionally dry. The applause of the congregation was no longer enough to fill the ache within her soul. She longed for someone to care for her, to notice that she, too, needed healing and support. Yet, the more she gave, the more the emptiness grew.

It wasn't just a matter of physical exhaustion; it was emotional depletion. Monica had sacrificed so much of herself to be the worship leader, the minister, the encourager — that she had lost sight of who she was outside of her role. Her identity had become tangled in her ministry, and her sense of worth was tied to what she could do for others. The problem was that the weight of others' expectations had begun to drown out her own needs.

The breaking point came when Monica made a courageous decision — one that shocked her church community. She stepped away from her leadership role, taking a sabbatical from ministry. For many, it seemed like an abrupt and inexplicable decision. How could she leave when her voice had been instrumental in leading so many to the Lord? But for Monica, it was the only option. She knew that if she didn't take a step back, she might lose herself entirely.

"I had to heal," she said, looking back on that difficult decision. "I had to find my voice outside of performance. I had to remember I was a daughter before I was a leader. That saved me."

Taking time off from ministry wasn't easy. It meant facing her struggles head-on, addressing the pain in her marriage, and seeking the help she needed. It meant allowing herself the space to grieve, to be vulnerable, and to finally acknowledge the emotional toll her role had taken on her. It meant realizing that her worth was not defined by her ability to lead worship, but by her identity as a beloved daughter of God.

As she took time to heal, Monica began to rebuild her life, piece by piece. She worked on her marriage, seeking counseling and opening up about the deep wounds that had formed over the years. She began to reconnect with her children, learning to be present with them, not as a leader, but as a mother who needed them just as much as they needed her.

And in that season of silence, she rediscovered her relationship with God. She learned to hear His voice outside the pressure of ministry, to receive His love without the expectation of performing for others. In the quiet moments, God began to sing over her once more, filling the empty spaces in her heart with His presence.

Through her journey, Monica realized that leadership in ministry wasn't about what she could give; it was about who she was. She had spent so long pouring herself out that she had forgotten the importance of being filled up. She learned that true ministry comes from a place of health, both spiritually and emotionally.

When Monica returned to ministry, it was with a renewed sense of purpose. She no longer sought the approval of others for her worth. Her identity as a daughter of God became the foundation of her leadership. She no longer felt the need to perform; instead, she led with authenticity and humility, knowing that she was deeply loved, not for what she did, but for who she was.

Monica's story is a reminder that even those who seem to have it all together may be silently suffering. It's a call to all leaders, and especially worship leaders, to remember that self-care is not selfish; it's essential. True strength comes from vulnerability, from taking the time to heal and find peace within oneself. Ministry, after all, is not about what we can do for others; it's about being rooted in God's love, so we can pour that love out to others in a way that is sustainable and life-giving.

Monica's breakthrough came when she chose to break the silence, to acknowledge her struggles, and to step into the healing she so desperately needed. And in doing so, she rediscovered her true voice — the one that comes from a place of wholeness, love, and grace.

The Way Forward
In life, we often find ourselves caught in a cycle of striving, where our worth feels tied to our performance, our ability to impress others, and the applause we receive in response. We may thrive in the spotlight, receiving accolades for our talents and contributions, but deep within, there's a pain that goes unnoticed. This pain often gets buried under the weight of expectations, both from others and from ourselves. But it's time to stop and confront that pain. It's time to acknowledge that God

cares more about your soul than your stage. He is not impressed with your performance; He is deeply concerned with the condition of your heart.

The Power of Honesty
True healing begins with honesty—not just with others, but first and foremost, with yourself. It's time to remove the mask, the one you wear so well—the mask of perfection, of strength, of "I'm fine." You don't have to pretend anymore. You don't have to carry the crushing weight of having it all together when your soul is quietly unraveling. There is courage in confession. There is strength in surrender. It is not weakness to admit that you're not okay—it is wisdom. It is the first step toward wholeness.

You were never created to live in fragments, constantly patching yourself up just enough to make it through the day while pouring out wholeness into others. That's not sustainable. That's not healthy. That's not God's design for you. There is a kind of compassion you extend so freely to others—grace, patience, empathy, forgiveness—but when will you offer that same compassion to yourself?

You deserve the same mercy you give away. You deserve a safe place to fall apart, to breathe, to heal. Stop disqualifying yourself from healing just because you're the one who's usually strong. Even the strongest have their breaking points. Even the most faithful servants need rest. And even the most compassionate hearts need comfort.

We live in a world that glorifies performance and perfection, yet it is in our most vulnerable moments that true strength emerges.

Vulnerability is not the absence of strength—it is the birthplace of it. When you are honest about your pain, your fears, your disappointments, and your doubts, you allow the light of truth to shine into the darkest corners of your heart. You make space for God to do what only He can do: restore, rebuild, and renew.

Healing is not linear. It is not tidy. It's not a quick fix or a motivational quote. Healing is messy. It requires patience. It demands courage. It asks you to sit with the uncomfortable, to feel what you've long buried, and to confront the parts of you you'd rather hide. But in that confrontation, in that sacred honesty, God meets you. Not with condemnation, but with compassion. Not with shame, but with love.

He doesn't ask you to clean yourself up before coming to Him. He simply asks you to come. As you are. Broken. Tired. Hurt. Confused. Because He already sees what's beneath the surface—and He still calls you beloved.

You don't have to perform for healing. You don't have to pretend your wounds don't hurt. You don't have to wear a smile when your soul is crying. What you do need is to be honest. Start there. Whisper the truth in your prayers. Confess the pain to someone safe. Allow yourself to feel again. That's not regression—it's redemption in process.

Honesty is how the walls come down. Honesty is how healing begins. And honesty is how freedom is found.

The Journey of Healing
Healing is not a linear path—it doesn't follow a straight line or a

predictable timeline. It's a winding road filled with highs and lows, progress and setbacks, clarity and confusion. Many times, we want healing to be quick, simple, and clean, but real healing is often slow, messy, and layered. It's not a one-time event but a process—an unfolding journey where you gradually become whole again.

This journey invites you to embrace every part of yourself—not just the polished or presentable parts, but also the broken, hurting, and hidden parts. Healing doesn't require perfection; it requires *presence*. It requires you to show up to your own life with honesty, vulnerability, and a willingness to let God meet you right where you are.

God never asked you to fix yourself before coming to Him. He knows every scar, every tear, every hidden struggle—and still, He draws near. He is not looking for perfection; He is looking for surrender. He is the Great Physician, and His healing touch doesn't just treat the symptoms—it transforms the heart.

There is often a strong temptation to rush through the healing process, especially in a world that celebrates performance over authenticity. You may feel pressure to "get over it," to be strong, to put on a smile, and to return to what feels familiar or functional. But true healing cannot be microwaved. It requires *space*. It requires *time*. It requires *grace*.

Sometimes healing means sitting quietly in the discomfort instead of escaping it. It means naming the pain rather than numbing it. It means stepping off the stage, out of the spotlight, or away from the noise to allow God to do deep, inner work that can't be seen by others—but is deeply felt in your soul.

Don't despise the seasons of stillness. Don't fear the moments when everything feels undone. Often, those are the very places where God is doing His most intimate and lasting work. Let Him touch the sore places. Let Him rewrite the stories you've believed about yourself. Let Him breathe life into the areas that feel dead or forgotten.

Healing is holy ground. It's where you learn that being whole isn't about being flawless—it's about being honest. It's about being connected again to the One who created you and allows you to flourish in His timing.

So be gentle with yourself. Trust the process. Release the urge to perform or to hurry. Healing doesn't always look like progress on the outside—it often looks like tears, rest, and quiet surrender. But with every step, no matter how small, you are moving closer to the heart of God and the wholeness He promises.

You don't have to walk this road alone. God walks with you—patiently, lovingly, and faithfully. And in His time, He will make all things new.

Finding Safe Spaces
In the journey of healing, few things are more vital than discovering and cultivating *safe spaces*—places where your soul can exhale, your heart can be honest, and your wounds can be gently tended to without fear or shame. These spaces become sacred ground, not because they are free of pain, but because they are full of grace. In a world that constantly demands performance, safe spaces are where the masks can come off, and your true self can breathe.

Safe spaces come in various forms, and each person may find them in different places depending on their story, personality, and spiritual walk. Yet, they all share a powerful commonality: they are environments where you are embraced, not for what you do, but for who you are. There is no need to pretend, to suppress, or to strive. You are permitted to feel, to falter, and to heal.

Therapy is one of the most structured forms of a safe space. It offers a professional, confidential, and non-judgmental environment where your pain is not minimized or ignored, but held with care. A therapist doesn't fix you—they help you understand, navigate, and make peace with your pain. They guide you into clarity, helping you uncover patterns, break cycles, and begin rebuilding from the inside out.

Friendship, when rooted in authenticity, becomes another healing space. These are the friends who don't need you to always have it together. They sit with you in your silence, they cry with you in your sorrow, and they celebrate even your smallest steps forward. True friends don't push you to move on before you're ready—they walk with you until you are.

Mentorship brings another layer of healing—a sense of direction and wisdom. Mentors offer more than encouragement; they offer perspective. Having walked similar roads, they carry a depth of understanding that can anchor you in times of confusion. Their testimonies remind you that healing is possible, that broken seasons don't last forever, and that scars can become signs of strength.

Then there is **solitude with God**, perhaps the deepest and most restorative safe space of all. It is here, in the quiet of your soul, that you are known completely and loved unconditionally. You don't have to explain yourself to God. You don't have to perform. You don't have to pretend. You can come undone in His presence—bring your questions, your anger, your sorrow, and your joy. God is your refuge, your hiding place, and your healer. In His presence, healing flows not from pressure but from rest.

Take intentional time to engage in these spaces. Make room in your life to *reflect*, to *release*, and to *rebuild*. Healing is not linear. It often comes in waves, in layers, in unexpected moments. Don't rush it. Don't judge it. Allow yourself the grace to be in process. And don't be afraid to cry. Don't be ashamed to grieve. Don't suppress the emotions you've buried for too long. Your tears are not a sign of weakness; they are a sacred language of the heart. They are how your soul says, *"I've carried too much for too long."* They water the soil of your healing and soften the ground for new growth.

Healing doesn't require perfection; it requires presence. Be present with yourself. Be present in the spaces that invite your honesty. And most of all, let God's presence envelop you, reminding you that no matter how broken you feel, you are never beyond repair.

Letting the Tears Lead You
Tears are not a sign of weakness—they are sacred drops of truth that reveal the hidden chambers of the soul. They hold stories, words are unable to express, burdens we've carried in silence, and pain we've tried to suppress. Sometimes, the very tears we've been avoiding are the keys God is trying to use to unlock our healing.

They are not an interruption to strength; they are the beginning of it.

Don't be ashamed to let them fall—even if it must happen in the quiet moments when no one else is watching. There's no shame in retreating to the secret place to cry, to wrestle, and to release. That hidden space becomes holy ground where God meets you, not in your polished performance, but in your brokenness. Each tear carries you closer to clarity, closer to wholeness, closer to Him.

Let your tears become more than emotional outbursts—let them be a **catalyst for change**. Let them speak of the trauma you're ready to confront, the memories you're finally brave enough to process, and the surrender you're willing to offer. With every tear, may you be emptied of pride, fear, and false strength—and filled instead with divine courage, insight, and resilience.

Healing is not linear. It is not always beautiful. It can feel like tearing down walls you built to protect yourself and confronting wounds you've tried to ignore. But it is in this raw, vulnerable process that you truly begin to heal. You don't come out the same person. You come out stronger, softer, wiser, and more in tune with who God created you to be.

The goal is not to return to the stage.

Not to impress others with how quickly you "bounced back" or how strong you appear. True healing does not require an audience. It requires intention, surrender, and time. The goal is not to perform, but to be transformed. To return not to function, but to wholeness—where your soul is at rest, your identity is rooted in truth, and your heart is healed.

Only from that place of peace can you authentically pour into others—not from depletion, but from overflow. You become a vessel of compassion because you know what it's like to be shattered. You carry grace because you remember how much you needed it. You love deeply because you've allowed yourself to be deeply healed.

So let the tears fall. Let them wash away the layers that no longer serve you. Let them baptize you into a new season. Let them lead you not into despair, but into the arms of the One who collects every tear and never wastes a single one. Your tears are not the end. They are the beginning of your becoming.

Embrace Your Humanity
The way forward is not through striving for flawlessness or pretending to have it all together. The path to wholeness begins with embracing your humanity—the truth that you are a person with limitations, emotions, struggles, and stories that have shaped who you are. You carry both light and shadow, strength and weakness, courage and fear. And yet, in all of this, you are deeply loved.

God never asked you to be perfect. He never expected you to live without wounds, doubts, or tears. Instead, He calls you to be *real*—to come before Him not with polished masks and rehearsed prayers, but with raw honesty, trembling vulnerability, and a heart willing to grow. He is not moved by performance, but by authenticity. It's not your strength that touches His heart, but your willingness to trust Him with your weakness.

So, pause. Breathe. Let go of the pressure to be everything for everyone. You were never designed to carry the weight of the world on your shoulders. You were not created to earn love through constant giving while silently draining yourself dry. God never intended for you to wear the mask of perfection or hide your pain beneath a smile. He longs for you to come as you are—wounded, weary, uncertain—and find rest in Him.

Permit yourself to heal. Not in haste, not on someone else's timeline, but at the pace your heart can bear. Extend grace to yourself. Grace, when you fall. Grace, when you feel broken. Grace, when the old wounds ache and the tears come unexpectedly. You don't have to have it all figured out. Healing is not linear—it's messy, sacred, and deeply personal.

And through it all, know this truth: God sees you. He sees beyond your doing and your striving. He sees your heart, your story, your quiet cries in the night. He knows your burdens. He counts your tears. And still, He calls you beloved. *Not for what you do—but for who you are.* In His eyes, you are enough. Not when you finally overcome. Not when you finally measure up. But *now*—even in your brokenness, you are enough.

As you walk the path of healing, hold tightly to the truth that you are not walking it alone. God is with you—closer than your breath, gentler than the morning sun. He walks beside you in the silence, in the ache, in the moments of doubt. His love surrounds you. His mercy restores you. His grace sustains you. And even when you can't feel Him, He is there—faithful, constant, and unwavering.

Yes, the journey may be hard. Some days may feel like battles. But this is not the end of your story. This is the sacred middle—the refining fire, the breaking that leads to blooming. In time, you will emerge not as the person who had it all together, but as someone who was remade in the furnace of grace. Stronger. Softer. Wiser. Whole.

And through it all, may you come to know the beauty of being human—deeply loved by a God who is not intimidated by your mess, but is glorified in your surrender.

CHAPTER 3
The Loneliness of the Mantle

Isolation as a Leader's Reality

Leadership, in its truest sense, often comes with a heavy burden of solitude. Those who step into positions of influence, authority, or responsibility frequently find themselves isolated. The mantle of leadership, though a calling, can feel like a solitary journey. While many may view leadership as a position of power and admiration, it often carries with it a sense of being set apart, misunderstood, and alone.

The Burden of Responsibility

Leadership is not merely a position of influence—it is a mantle of responsibility. At its core, to lead is to bear the weight of others' well-being. It is to navigate not only one's personal journey but also to chart a course for many, often in uncharted waters. Every decision a leader makes ripples outward, impacting families, organizations, communities, and sometimes entire nations. The burden of knowing that one's choices can change the trajectory of life is not a light one; it is heavy, complex, and often lonely.

The Silent Weight of Decision-Making

In times of crisis, this burden intensifies. The leader must make hard choices—often between two difficult options—knowing that not everyone will understand, and many will not agree. In such moments, emotions must be managed, pressure absorbed, and clarity maintained, even when the path ahead is unclear. While followers may look for reassurance and vision, the leader must wrestle privately with uncertainty and fear. This creates an emotional toll that is invisible to the outside world. Many see the authority, the platform, and the respect, but few perceive the internal conflicts and the sleepless nights that come with making decisions that cannot please everyone.

The Inevitable Isolation
The higher one climbs in leadership, the lonelier the journey can become. Isolation often comes not by choice, but by necessity. To serve a broader mission, leaders must detach from their personal preferences and filter their decisions through the lens of what is best for the whole. This objectivity—while essential—can come at the cost of personal connection. Genuine friendships may become harder to maintain, not because the leader lacks love or loyalty, but because trust becomes more complicated and vulnerability more costly.

Many leaders find themselves surrounded by people, yet profoundly alone. They may long to confide in someone but hesitate for fear that their honesty could be misinterpreted, misused, or undermine their credibility. The very people they serve may admire or even revere them—but not truly know them. This isolation can be emotionally draining, especially when leaders themselves are struggling, yet feel compelled to appear strong for the sake of those they lead.

Suppression of Self
Another dimension of this burden is the subtle but persistent suppression of personal needs. Leaders often silence their own

desires, dreams, and emotional struggles in order to stay focused on the collective mission. They learn to wear masks of composure while burying their personal battles. In the name of discipline and vision, they learn to downplay their humanity. Over time, this can lead to a disconnection not only from others but also from themselves.

In a world that increasingly demands authenticity and emotional intelligence from its leaders, this internal conflict becomes even more pronounced. How does a leader remain transparent without being perceived as weak? How can they be empathetic without compromising decisiveness? How do they maintain relational warmth without losing the edge of leadership clarity? These are the tightropes leaders walk every day.

The Need for Safe Spaces
To survive and thrive under the burden of responsibility, leaders must intentionally cultivate safe spaces. They need places and people where they can remove the mask, lay down the burden, and be seen not as a title or position, but as a human being. Mentors, counselors, close confidants, and times of solitude with God or personal reflection can serve as lifelines. These sacred spaces allow leaders to process their emotions, renew their strength, and recalibrate their purpose without judgment or expectation.

A Sacred Weight
Leadership, when viewed rightly, is not a badge of superiority—it is a sacred stewardship. It is the call to carry others, sometimes at great personal cost. But even as leaders bear this weight, they must not forget their need for grace, restoration, and human

connection. To lead effectively over the long haul, leaders must learn to balance vision with vulnerability, discipline with compassion, and responsibility with rest.

Because even those who carry others need someone to carry them.

The Paradox of Being Surrounded Yet Alone

One of the most silent struggles in leadership is loneliness—the kind that doesn't stem from the absence of people, but from a disconnect that exists even in a crowded room. This paradox is both subtle and profound: the more responsibility a leader carries, the more surrounded they become by people, yet the more isolated they often feel. It's not about being physically alone, but emotionally and psychologically distanced from others.

Leaders are frequently placed on pedestals—seen as visionaries, problem-solvers, motivators, and steady anchors in the midst of crisis. They are expected to radiate strength, clarity, and composure, especially in times of uncertainty. Vulnerability, hesitation, or emotional transparency are often seen as cracks in the armor—risks that could weaken their credibility or the confidence others have in their leadership.

As a result, many leaders wear emotional masks. They suppress their fears, bottle up their doubts, and smile through the weight of heavy decisions, all while wrestling silently with personal battles no one sees. It becomes difficult, even dangerous, to let people in. Confiding in someone might seem like risking respect. Admitting struggle may be mistaken for incompetence. The image must remain intact, even when the person behind it is cracking.

This internal dissonance breeds isolation. Leaders may find themselves surrounded by people who admire them, depend on them, and even cheer them—but rarely truly know them. The irony is that their strength becomes their solitude. The very attributes that elevate them also create barriers: decisiveness can be mistaken for aloofness; confidence can be interpreted as detachment; high standards can create fear rather than connection.

Moreover, those under a leader's care often hesitate to approach them with honesty. Subordinates or team members may withhold their own vulnerabilities, assuming the leader wouldn't understand, or worse, wouldn't care. The leader, in turn, absorbs the burdens of others while quietly carrying their own, often with nowhere to lay them down. Friendships become complex; trust must be weighed carefully. Genuine companionship is hard to find when people filter their words around you or seek your position rather than your personhood.

Yet, at the heart of every leader is a human being—longing to be understood, supported, and accepted without the title. Behind the strategic mind is a heart that aches for companionship without pretense. Beneath the courageous front is someone who needs encouragement, grace, and space to breathe without performance.

This paradox calls for a reevaluation of how we view leadership. True strength lies not in pretending to be invincible but in knowing when to be vulnerable. It's in building safe circles where honesty is welcomed and authenticity isn't punished. Leaders need mentors, peers, and sometimes even counselors—not because they are weak, but because they are wise enough to know that strength without support becomes a burden too great to bear.

In breaking the myth of the untouchable leader, we make room for a new kind of leadership—one that leads with both head and heart, one that finds power in humility and connection, and one that recognizes that even the strongest shoulders need to be carried sometimes.

Spiritual Isolation: The Unspoken Battle

Leadership can be a profoundly rewarding calling, but it is not without its hidden costs—chief among them is **spiritual isolation**. Beneath the external image of strength, clarity, and guidance that leaders are often expected to project, there can exist a silent battle within the soul—a battle between personal vulnerability and public expectation, between inner questions and the outward demand for unwavering faith.

In times of crisis or uncertainty, people instinctively look to their leaders for stability. They lean on them for hope, clarity, direction, and answers. But what happens when the leader themselves is navigating fog? What happens when the one expected to light the way is trying to find their own footing in the dark?

This unspoken struggle is where spiritual isolation begins.

The Pressure to Be Unshakable

Sometimes, what a leader needs is not advice, but a trained ear. **Coaches help leaders reflect, refine their thinking, and rediscover their inner compass.** Counselors, on the other hand, especially in faith-based or spiritual communities, are often placed on a pedestal. They are expected to be the unwavering example—to have the vision, the answers, and the spiritual stamina to weather any storm. This idealized expectation, however, can be a double-edged sword. While it may inspire confidence in others, it often leaves little room for the leader's own humanity.

The truth is that **leaders wrestle with doubt,** too. They face moments of deep questioning, fatigue, and even spiritual dryness. But because vulnerability is often perceived as weakness, especially from those in authority, leaders may suppress their struggles. They feel the weight of others' dependence, which creates a deep sense of responsibility that says, *"I must not break. I cannot let them see me struggle."* Over time, this internal suppression becomes isolation—not just from people, but from spiritual lifelines.

Disconnected from the Well

Spiritual isolation is more than being alone—it is the sense of being **disconnected from God, from purpose, and from the very source of one's strength.** The demands of leadership often mean pouring out to others constantly—teaching, praying, encouraging, counseling, and leading. Yet without intentional replenishment, leaders can become spiritually dehydrated. They continue serving while running on empty.

When a leader feels they must always give but cannot receive—or feels ashamed to admit when they are running low—it becomes a dangerous cycle. They continue outward duties while inwardly feeling dry, distant, and even disillusioned. The disconnect from spiritual intimacy deepens. It's not that they no longer believe; it's that they no longer feel safe enough to wrestle openly with what they believe.

The Loneliness of Hidden Battles
One of the greatest dangers of spiritual isolation is that **leaders begin to suffer in silence**. They bear the pressure of expectations without a safe space to unburden their hearts. The fear that transparency will be misunderstood—or worse, weaponized—keeps them locked in silence. And so, the inner war rages on in private.

They may smile in public but cry secretly. They may preach sermons while feeling spiritually numb. They may counsel others while silently wondering if anyone truly sees them. And though surrounded by people, they can feel profoundly alone.

Reclaiming Connection
So how does a leader break free from this cycle of spiritual isolation?

1. **Safe Spaces for Vulnerability**: Leaders need relationships where they can be fully human—where they can take off the mantle of leadership and simply be a child of God. Trusted mentors, spiritual directors, or peers who understand the weight of leadership can be a lifeline. Vulnerability, in the right environment, can be deeply healing.
2. **Permission to Rest and Recharge**: Constant output without input leads to burnout. Leaders must carve out time for spiritual replenishment—time alone with God not for sermon preparation, but for soul restoration. Time to sit, be still, and hear again the gentle whisper of God's presence.
3. **Honest Conversations with God**: Leaders must be reminded that God is not intimidated by their doubts, frustrations, or questions. The Psalms are full of raw,

unfiltered conversations with God. Returning to that place of honesty in prayer reconnects the leader to intimacy, not performance.
4. **The Power of Community**: Spiritual isolation shrinks in the presence of real, grace-filled community. Finding or building a community where authenticity is celebrated—not penalized—can restore what isolation has stolen.

Strength in Surrender

True strength in leadership is not the absence of weakness—it's the courage to **face weakness without shame**, to acknowledge need without fear of rejection, and to lead from a place of dependence on God, not personal perfection. Spiritual isolation may be an unspoken battle, but it must not be fought alone.

If you're a leader walking this path, know this: *You are not failing because you struggle. You are human because you struggle.* And in your most fragile moments, God's grace is still sufficient. Sometimes, the most powerful thing a leader can do is not to pretend to have it all together—but to **humbly return to the well**, receive, and then lead again—from a place of overflow, not emptiness.

The Importance of Authentic Connections

Leadership often projects an image of unwavering strength, decisiveness, and resilience. To those on the outside, leaders may appear impenetrable—always in control, always confident. However, the reality beneath the surface is often much more complex. Leadership can be lonely. The responsibility of decision-making, the weight of expectations, and the pressure to consistently perform can slowly erode a leader's sense of connection to others, creating a silent but deep emotional and relational gap.

This isolation, if left unchecked, can lead to burnout, discouragement, and even moral failure. That is why authentic connection is not a luxury for leaders—it is a necessity.

True leadership is not just about standing tall in public; it's also about being able to kneel in private. Leaders must be intentional about seeking out and maintaining relationships where they are allowed to be fully human—where they can be vulnerable without judgment, express uncertainty without condemnation, and receive encouragement without strings attached.

Building a strong and authentic support system is foundational to a leader's long-term well-being and effectiveness. This network might include wise mentors who offer seasoned counsel, trusted peers who provide mutual accountability, or spiritual advisors who help nurture the leader's inner life. These individuals serve as mirrors, reflecting truth, offering perspective, and reminding the leader that they are not alone in their journey.

Authentic connections also create a buffer against the dangers of ego and pride. When a leader surrounds themselves with people who love them enough to speak the truth—even when it's uncomfortable—they are more likely to remain grounded and self-aware. These relationships keep the leader aligned with their values and help them lead with integrity and humility.

Moreover, authentic connection fosters emotional resilience. Well-connected leaders are better equipped to navigate crises, manage stress, and bounce back from setbacks. They don't carry the weight of their responsibilities alone; they have shoulders to lean on, voices to uplift them, and hearts that understand.

In a culture that often idolizes self-reliance, it is courageous for a leader to admit their need for others. But this kind of courage breeds a different, more sustainable form of strength—one rooted not in isolation, but in community.

Ultimately, leaders who cultivate authentic relationships are not only healthier and happier—they are also more impactful. Their leadership flows from a place of wholeness, and that wholeness becomes a gift to those they serve.

The Role of Self-Care and Reflection
Leadership can be deeply fulfilling, but it is also demanding—emotionally, mentally, physically, and spiritually. One of the most overlooked yet essential components of sustainable leadership is self-care and intentional reflection. Leaders are often expected to be strong, available, and responsive to the needs of others, which can lead to chronic neglect of their own well-being. However, effective leadership is not sustainable without consistently nurturing the self.

Self-care is not a luxury; it is a leadership responsibility. When leaders fail to attend to their own needs, they not only risk burnout but also diminish their capacity to lead with empathy, clarity, and resilience. Leadership rooted in constant output without renewal will inevitably lead to exhaustion, emotional detachment, and impaired judgment. Therefore, it is imperative that leaders recognize self-care as a discipline that fuels longevity and effectiveness.

Reflection is a vital part of this self-care process. Taking intentional pauses to assess one's motivations, emotional health, decisions, and spiritual alignment helps leaders maintain integrity and clarity. Without reflection, leaders can easily drift into autopilot, where reactive patterns replace thoughtful leadership. By stepping back to reflect, leaders gain perspective, recalibrate their purpose, and make wiser, more grounded decisions.

Self-care might involve:
- **Scheduled solitude**: Time alone to simply be—away from demands, screens, and noise.
- **Journaling or spiritual meditation**: Processing emotions, victories, challenges, and lessons.
- **Physical wellness**: Prioritizing sleep, nutrition, and exercise to maintain physical energy.
- **Emotional boundaries**: Saying "no" when needed and creating space for personal time.
- **Engaging in life-giving activities**: Whether it's reading, walking, music, or time with loved ones—leaders need joy to refuel.

Moreover, spiritual self-care is especially important for values-driven and faith-based leaders. Regular time in prayer, scripture reading, or contemplation helps leaders remain rooted in their deeper calling and aligned with divine guidance. Spiritual renewal fosters humility, courage, and compassion—qualities that are essential for impactful leadership.

Leaders who are intentional about self-care and reflection not only model healthy boundaries to their teams but also create cultures of well-being and balance. They lead from a place of wholeness, not depletion. They are more emotionally available, less reactive under stress, and more present in their relationships. Ultimately, a well-nurtured soul is a leader's greatest asset.

Breaking the Cycle of Isolation

Leadership is often romanticized as a position of strength, vision, and unshakable confidence. Yet, beneath the surface, many leaders quietly grapple with a profound sense of isolation. The very role that calls them to serve, guide, and inspire others can sometimes leave them feeling disconnected, unsupported, and emotionally depleted. This cycle of isolation is not inevitable, but breaking free from it requires a deliberate and courageous act: intentionality.

Intentional Connection Over Accidental Loneliness

The antidote to isolation is not merely being around people, it is cultivating meaningful and trustworthy relationships. Leaders must be intentional about creating a personal support system that nurtures their inner life, not just their professional image. This involves identifying people with whom they can be fully themselves, beyond the title, the pressure, and the public face.

Intentional connection means scheduling time with mentors, peers, counselors, or even friends who can listen without judgment. It means showing up in spaces not to lead, but to learn, rest, and be known. It requires stepping away from the performance mindset and embracing the reality that vulnerability is not a weakness but a doorway to genuine strength.

The Power of Vulnerability

One of the main barriers to connection is the fear of vulnerability. Leaders often feel the pressure to have it all together, fearing that any sign of struggle will diminish their credibility. However, true leadership is not about pretending to be invulnerable; it's about modeling authenticity.

When leaders permit themselves to admit they're tired, confused, or even afraid, they create a ripple effect of honesty within their teams and organizations. Vulnerability disarms shame and invites trust. It reminds others—and the leader themselves—that being human is not a liability in leadership, but an asset.

You Are Not Alone in the Struggle
Isolation feeds on the lie that "no one else understands." The truth is that many leaders silently battle the same challenges: fatigue, emotional burnout, imposter syndrome, and relational drift. When these struggles remain hidden, they intensify. But when shared, they lose their power to isolate.

Creating or joining peer communities, leadership cohorts, or even informal gatherings with fellow leaders can provide the mutual encouragement that is often missing. These spaces offer empathy, shared wisdom, and the healing knowledge that, while leadership may feel lonely, it is not a solitary path. Others are walking similar roads—and they, too, are seeking companionship along the way.

From Isolation to Flourishing
Breaking the cycle of isolation is not only about emotional survival—it's about personal and professional flourishing. When leaders are rooted in relationships that nurture their souls, they are more resilient, more creative, and more capable of making wise, compassionate decisions. They lead not from emptiness but from overflow.

This also impacts the culture they create. Leaders who model healthy connections foster environments of trust, openness, and mutual care. Their teams become more collaborative, empathetic, and grounded—not in fear, but in shared purpose.

Leading With Authenticity and Grounded Wisdom
In conclusion, leadership does not have to mean standing alone on a pedestal, isolated from those who support, challenge, and humanize you. The most enduring and impactful leaders are not those who portray an image of perfection or invincibility, but those who choose to lead from a place of authenticity—open about their humanity, grounded in their values, and secure enough to admit what they don't know.

True leadership is not a spotlight; it is a bridge. It's about guiding others while remaining connected to your own soul and the people you serve. It means being real, relatable, and rooted. It's the ability to inspire without pretending, to correct without condemning, and to influence without manipulating. This kind of leadership doesn't rely on power plays or distant admiration but earns trust through transparency and consistency.

By embracing vulnerability, leaders invite others into their journey—not as spectators, but as partners. Vulnerability does not weaken a leader's authority; it enriches it. It builds trust, creates safe spaces for growth, and reminds everyone that leadership is not about hierarchy, but about shared purpose.

Authentic leaders also recognize the importance of nurturing their inner world. They prioritize spiritual, emotional, and mental well-being—not as an afterthought, but as a foundation for sustainable impact. When a leader's soul is nourished, their leadership becomes more intuitive, compassionate, and resilient. Self-care is not selfish; it is stewardship. A depleted leader cannot pour into others effectively. But a whole, rested, and spiritually rooted leader can pour with grace, discernment, and wisdom.

Moreover, grounded leaders intentionally surround themselves with wise counsel, life-giving relationships, and accountability. They resist the temptation of self-reliance and understand that isolation is not a badge of honor, but a breeding ground for burnout, pride, and poor decisions. They lean into the strength of community, drawing wisdom from diverse perspectives and courage from collective strength.

In the end, the most transformative leaders are not those who try to carry everything alone, but those who know how to draw strength from togetherness. They lead from within and from among—not above. Their wisdom is not detached or idealistic, but forged in the fires of experience, humility, and connection.

Because strength is not found in perfection—it is found in presence. And wisdom is not proven by how much you know, but by how well you love, listen, and lead in community.

Trust Issues—Who Can a Leader Talk To?
Trust is the bedrock of any meaningful relationship, and for leaders, it is both a strength and a vulnerability. However, as a leader rises to greater levels of influence and responsibility, the very dynamic of trust becomes more complicated. The deeper a leader's role, the smaller their circle of trust tends to become. The burden of leadership often creates an environment where vulnerability is seen as a weakness, not a strength. For those at the

top, the question of whom they can confide in becomes not just relevant but critical.

The Paradox of Leadership and Trust

As leaders, whether in business, ministry, politics, or community service, the calling is noble, but the journey is riddled with complexity. Leadership is often romanticized as a position of influence, control, and respect. But beneath the surface, many leaders silently wrestle with the crushing burden of expectations. The weight of decisions, the responsibility for people's well-being, and the constant pressure to deliver results can become emotionally and spiritually overwhelming.

One of the greatest ironies of leadership is that the higher you rise, the lonelier it can become. Leadership is inherently relational, yet many leaders find themselves emotionally isolated. This isolation is often not due to a lack of people around them but a lack of people they can truly trust. With every promotion, accolade, or position of visibility, there comes a quiet caution: *"Who can I confide in without it being used against me?"* Vulnerability, though a mark of humanity, begins to feel like a liability. The stakes are too high. One misplaced confession can spiral into gossip, manipulation, or betrayal.

The paradox is that while trust is foundational to effective leadership, it is also one of the most challenging aspects to navigate. Leaders are expected to build trust with others—to be transparent, authentic, and approachable—yet they often find themselves unable to trust in return. The fear of being misunderstood, judged, or discredited keeps many leaders in a prison of emotional self-preservation.

To cope, many adopt a hardened persona. They build emotional walls and project an image of infallibility—always composed, always in control, never shaken. This image may temporarily protect them from criticism or attack, but over time, it can erode their own well-being. Leaders who cannot express their doubts, fears, or failures begin to carry an unsustainable emotional weight. Burnout becomes likely. Compassion fatigue sets in. Their leadership becomes more mechanical than heartfelt.

This facade also creates disconnection. Team members, congregants, or employees may admire their strength but feel distant from their humanity. And when followers feel their leader is untouchable or disconnected, genuine loyalty and unity begin to erode. People may respect a leader's ability, but they connect with their authenticity. The very mask designed to preserve authority ends up undermining influence.

Yet, the answer is not reckless vulnerability. Leaders do not need to pour out their every fear or struggle to everyone. Wisdom in vulnerability is key. Trusted, mature confidants—mentors, counselors, spiritual advisors—are invaluable. Safe spaces must be intentionally cultivated, where leaders can process pain, ask hard questions, and receive truth without fear of exploitation.

Moreover, leaders must embrace the truth that being human does not disqualify them; it qualifies them. Admitting weakness doesn't mean a loss of respect; it often deepens it when done in the right context. It shows courage, humility, and integrity. It builds a culture where others, too, feel safe to be real, to grow, and to fail forward.

True strength in leadership is not about always having the right answers; it's about having the courage to lead even when you don't. It's about creating a rhythm of trust where authenticity can exist without fear, and where leadership is not a mask, but a mission lived out with humility, wisdom, and grace.

The Shrinking Circle of Trust
As leaders ascend to higher levels of influence and responsibility, one of the paradoxical realities they face is the gradual shrinking of their circle of trust. While their networks may grow, and their influence may spread widely, the number of individuals they can truly confide in often diminishes. Leadership is not merely about vision and decision-making; it comes with a unique weight that few can fully comprehend unless they have walked the same path.

The higher a leader rises, the lonelier the summit can become. At the top, the air is thinner—not just literally in terms of position, but metaphorically in terms of companionship. Many around them may admire their leadership or respect their authority, but admiration is not the same as understanding. It can be difficult to find someone who can relate to the internal conflicts, high-stakes decisions, moral dilemmas, and emotional toll that come with leading others. This often leaves leaders with the disorienting feeling of being surrounded by people, yet profoundly alone.

Within an organization, subordinates may view their leader with awe or caution. Even when a leader desires open dialogue, those under their leadership may struggle to engage with them as equals. The power dynamics can suppress honest conversations. Employees might tailor their words, withhold criticism, or overpraise—either to stay in good favor or to avoid potential conflict. This filtered communication creates an emotional and relational barrier, further isolating the leader from genuine feedback and support.

Peers—those who share a similar rank or influence—should, in theory, be the most relatable companions. However, the reality is often more complicated. In competitive environments, peer relationships can be tainted by rivalry, political maneuvering, or hidden agendas. Trusting a peer can feel like exposing one's vulnerabilities to someone who might later use them as leverage. Even when there is goodwill, the pressure of comparison and the ambition to stay ahead can subtly erode the foundation of mutual support.

Moreover, as leaders gain prominence, they become targets of increased scrutiny. Every word, action, or decision is weighed heavily—not just by the public or stakeholders, but also by those within their inner circle. The possibility of betrayal becomes a very real concern. Trusted confidants may shift allegiance if opportunities arise. A private conversation can be leaked. A moment of transparency can be weaponized. Leaders, having perhaps been burned in the past, begin to carry the burden of suspicion and self-censorship. The result? A cautious withdrawal from intimacy, even in relationships that once felt secure.

This shrinking circle of trust doesn't always stem from paranoia; often, it's the result of painful experience. Loyalty is precious, and betrayal—especially when it comes from someone close—leaves deep scars. Over time, leaders may feel the need to compartmentalize, sharing bits of themselves selectively, if at all. The cost of being too open becomes higher than the comfort of being fully known.

However, leaders cannot thrive in total isolation. Those who endure and lead well for the long haul often find ways to counter this dynamic. They seek out safe spaces—whether through mentors, spiritual advisors, professional coaches, or long-time friends outside their organization—where they can be vulnerable without fear of repercussion. They may invest intentionally in cultivating a small group of trusted individuals who have proven their loyalty, confidentiality, and wisdom over time. And perhaps most importantly, they come to terms with the reality that while the circle may be small, its strength matters more than its size.

In the end, the shrinking circle of trust is not a flaw in leadership, but a natural consequence of increased visibility and responsibility. The challenge for any leader is not to resent it, but to manage it with discernment, humility, and intentionality. Because in a world where many want to be close to power, few are willing or able to carry the weight of true trust.

The Loneliness of Leadership
Leadership, for all its influence and visibility, can be an incredibly isolating journey. The higher one climbs on the ladder of responsibility, the smaller the circle of trust becomes. What begins as a vibrant network of peers and confidants gradually shrinks into a tight, cautious inner circle—or, in some cases, none at all. This narrowing of emotional and relational space is not often spoken of, but it's one of the most taxing burdens that leaders carry.

Isolation is not just the absence of people; it is the absence of those with whom one can be truly honest. Leaders are expected to embody strength, composure, and decisiveness. They are the ones others look to in moments of crisis. They are expected to "have it together," to set the tone, to rise above the storm. But what happens when the storm rages inside the leader? When they face self-doubt, fear, or fatigue? Often, there is no safe space to share these vulnerabilities without risking perception, credibility, or authority.

The burden of always being "on" can lead to profound emotional fatigue. Leaders may find themselves pouring endlessly into others while receiving little in return. Over time, this imbalance becomes draining—not just physically, but spiritually and psychologically. It becomes harder to feel seen, harder to feel understood. In an environment where everyone expects you to have the answers, admitting that you're struggling can feel like a betrayal of your role.

In reality, leadership often demands the suppression of the very qualities that make us human—fear, confusion, grief, and even joy at times—when those emotions seem out of step with the needs of the team or the optics of the moment. This kind of suppression builds up. It festers beneath polished speeches and well-managed appearances. Eventually, the leader may feel like they are carrying the weight of an entire organization or mission on their shoulders, silently and alone.

And because society often defines success by outcomes—profits, impact, growth—few stop to consider the emotional and psychological cost it took to get there. The sleepless nights. The moral dilemmas. The personal sacrifices. The relationships strained or lost along the way. To the world, the leader is strong, admirable, and unshakable. But to the leader themselves, the mirror might tell a story of exhaustion, disconnection, and deep inner weariness.

Burnout is not just about being tired; it is about being emptied. A leader can be surrounded by people yet feel utterly alone. They can lead meetings, cast vision, and motivate others while internally wrestling with despair, doubt, or disillusionment. And when leaders feel that they cannot show weakness, they suppress it until it becomes destructive—manifesting as depression, anxiety, irritability, or detachment.

This is why leadership must be supported, not only through strategic tools and professional development, but through genuine emotional and relational accountability. Leaders need safe spaces—mentors, coaches, trusted friends—where they can remove the mask without fear. They need room to process, reflect, and be vulnerable. Because behind every strong leader is a human being with limits, emotions, and a soul in need of care.

In the end, leadership doesn't have to be lonely. But it often is—unless we begin to shift the culture around what strength in leadership truly means. True strength is not the absence of weakness, but the courage to acknowledge it, to seek support, and to walk with humility even in high places.

The Dangers of Bottling Up
Bottling up emotions and fears is more than just a personal burden—it's a silent saboteur of effective leadership. When leaders suppress their inner struggles, believing they must always appear strong, composed, and unfazed, they place themselves under immense psychological strain. This self-imposed pressure doesn't just impact their mental health; it compromises the very essence of good leadership—clarity, connection, and authenticity.

A leader who believes they cannot confide in anyone may begin to operate from a place of fear, not wisdom. Decisions that should be based on careful thought and sound judgment become filtered through the lens of anxiety, insecurity, or even pride. The result? Choices that may be reactive instead of proactive, self-protective rather than strategic, or overly rigid to avoid vulnerability. Over time, this can create a leadership style that feels erratic, controlling, or overly defensive, which can erode confidence in their vision and direction.

Moreover, bottling up emotions doesn't stay hidden forever. Internal pressure eventually leaks out—whether through bursts of anger, withdrawal, passive aggression, or burnout. Leaders who don't process and release their emotions in healthy ways risk becoming emotionally numb or overwhelmed. This emotional volatility can affect how they interact with others, leading to strained communication and relational breakdowns within their team or organization.

When a leader consistently hides their struggles, their team may begin to perceive them as unapproachable or out of touch. Employees might hesitate to share their own concerns or ideas, fearing that vulnerability isn't welcome or that their voices won't be heard. Over time, this erodes psychological safety—the foundation of team trust and innovation. What emerges is a culture where silence replaces openness, and assumptions replace dialogue.

Furthermore, when leaders isolate themselves emotionally, they lose access to one of the most vital resources in leadership: the wisdom, support, and perspective of others. No one leads effectively in a vacuum. Strong leadership is built on community—on advisors, mentors, peers, and trusted confidants who help leaders stay grounded, accountable, and human.

To avoid the dangers of bottling up, leaders must cultivate intentional spaces for emotional processing—whether through mentorship, counseling, spiritual guidance, or trusted peer relationships. Emotional intelligence isn't a weakness; it's a leadership superpower. Vulnerability, when paired with wisdom, doesn't diminish authority—it enhances credibility and deepens connection.

In a world that often rewards image over substance, it takes courage to lead with honesty. But leaders who learn to speak up, open up, and reach out will find themselves more resilient, more relatable, and ultimately, more effective.

Finding the Right People to Confide In
Leadership can be an isolating journey. The higher you climb, the fewer people there are around you who truly understand the weight you carry. With decisions that affect many, expectations that never cease, and responsibilities that often reach beyond the workplace into personal life, leaders face unique internal battles—ones that require safe, judgment-free spaces to process emotions, fears, and doubts.

So, who can a leader talk to?

Not everyone. In fact, not most people. A leader cannot afford to be emotionally vulnerable in every space or with every ear. But **every leader needs someone**—someone they can be real with. Someone they can talk to when the pressure mounts, the vision becomes unclear, or the weight of responsibility feels overwhelming.

This doesn't mean airing all personal and professional struggles publicly or with subordinates. It means finding **intentional, confidential, and safe relationships** that offer what public platforms and team meetings cannot: perspective, empathy, truth, and healing.

1. Mentors and Advisors
A mentor is often someone who has walked the same or similar path and bears the scars of experience. They know the terrain. Their wisdom is not theoretical; it is lived. Such individuals can help a leader see beyond the fog of the moment. They offer not only solutions but also stories—reminders that even giants stumble but rise again. A good mentor doesn't feed ego; they foster growth.

2. Professional Coaches and Counselors
Some are equipped to help process emotional wounds, stress, or deeper psychological burdens. Unlike casual friends, these professionals provide structured support, helping leaders develop coping tools, improve self-awareness, and maintain mental and emotional resilience.

3. Trusted Friends Who "Get It"
Not all friendships are created equally. A trusted friend, particularly one who understands the demands and dynamics of leadership—can be a lifeline. This friend doesn't see the leader as a title or role but as a person. They listen without trying to fix, offer presence more than platitudes, and remind the leader that they are more than their position.

However, boundaries still matter. Not every friend is suitable for every conversation. Leaders must wisely discern which friends have the maturity and capacity to handle their vulnerabilities with care and confidentiality.

4. Spiritual Directors and Faith Leaders

For those with spiritual convictions, faith can be an anchor in turbulent seasons. Prayer, scripture, and godly counsel from a pastor, spiritual director, or faith-based mentor can bring not only clarity but deep inner peace. **Sometimes, talking to God becomes the most honest and healing form of confession.** In spiritual circles, the wisdom of someone who can guide without legalism or bias is priceless.

5. The Importance of Intentional Effort

Such relationships don't happen by accident. Leaders must be **deliberate** in seeking them out. It requires humility to admit you need help, courage to reach out, and discernment to know who can truly be trusted. Ask:

- Does this person have a track record of discretion?
- Do they show wisdom, not just sympathy?
- Can they challenge me without undermining me?
- Do they genuinely care for me, not just my position?

Finding the right people to confide in is not a luxury for leaders, it's a necessity. Without these trusted connections, leaders risk burnout, emotional isolation, and poor decision-making. But with the right circle, they can stay grounded, make better choices, and lead from a place of strength and authenticity.

The Importance of Vulnerability for Effective Leadership
In today's evolving leadership landscape, vulnerability is no longer a weakness to be hidden, it is a strength to be embraced. Contrary to outdated notions of leadership that equate strength with stoicism and infallibility, effective leadership now requires authenticity, emotional intelligence, and the courage to be vulnerable.

Vulnerability builds trust. When leaders allow themselves to be open and transparent—whether it's acknowledging a mistake, expressing uncertainty, or sharing personal experiences, they foster a sense of safety within their teams. People are far more inclined to follow leaders they can relate to, not those who pretend to be untouchable. By showing vulnerability in appropriate ways, leaders become more human, approachable, and real. This humanization cultivates trust and deepens relational bonds, which are essential for any cohesive, high-performing team.

Admitting imperfections earns respect. No one expects a leader to be perfect. In fact, when leaders act as though they are, it can create distance and distrust. Teams respect leaders who can admit when they're wrong, who can say, "I don't know," and who are willing to learn from others. This humility not only models a culture of growth and learning, but it also encourages others to step up, contribute ideas, and take ownership—knowing that mistakes won't be met with shame but seen as opportunities for development.

Vulnerability invites collaboration. When leaders are willing to share their struggles or uncertainties, it opens the door for support and creative input. Instead of carrying the weight of leadership alone, vulnerable leaders create space for dialogue and collaboration. This openness often leads to innovative solutions and stronger team cohesion. Team members feel valued not just for their work, but for their perspectives and their willingness to walk alongside their leader through challenges.

Emotional release leads to clarity. Leaders are not immune to pressure, stress, or emotional fatigue. Bottling it all up for the sake of appearing "strong" can lead to burnout or poor decision-making. Vulnerability provides a necessary release valve. When leaders share what they're going through—whether with a trusted advisor, a mentor, or even with their team—it helps them unburden emotionally. This, in turn, refreshes their spirit and enables them to lead with renewed energy and clearer thinking.

It fosters a culture of psychological safety. Vulnerable leadership sets the tone for the rest of the organization. When a leader demonstrates that it's okay to speak up, to be honest about struggles, and to ask for help, it encourages others to do the same. This cultivates a culture of psychological safety where people are not afraid to take risks, voice concerns, or admit when they need support. Such environments are more adaptive, creative, and resilient.

Vulnerability is not about oversharing or being emotionally unstable. It is about authenticity, courage, and wisdom, the willingness to be seen as you are, while still carrying the vision and responsibility of leadership. When used wisely, vulnerability doesn't undermine authority; it enhances it. Leaders who embrace vulnerability lead not just with their heads, but with their hearts—and that kind of leadership leaves a lasting impact.

The Leader's Need for Balance
Leadership is a weighty responsibility, one that often isolates those who carry it. The higher a person climbs in influence and authority, the more complex the question becomes: *Who can I trust?* At its core, this question is not just about safeguarding information or avoiding betrayal—it is about balance. The balance between vulnerability and discernment, between transparency and discretion, and between relational closeness and professional distance.

For any leader, the ability to trust is not a luxury; it is a necessity. Without trust, leadership becomes an emotionally barren road marked by suspicion, guardedness, and deep loneliness. Over time, this isolation can drain even the most gifted and resilient leaders of the confidence and emotional strength required to lead effectively. The very qualities that once propelled them into leadership—vision, charisma, decisiveness—can begin to erode under the weight of internal solitude.

Yet, trust must be exercised wisely. Leaders are stewards of sensitive information, strategic decisions, and the morale of those they lead. They cannot afford to be careless with their words or overly casual with their confidants. But being cautious does not mean being closed. True leadership requires learning how to identify safe spaces—relationships where authenticity is not just allowed but welcomed.

To maintain balance, leaders must intentionally cultivate a support system beyond their positional responsibilities. Trusted mentors, friends, spouses, or faith-based relationships can serve as vital lifelines. These relationships are not about strategic advantage but about emotional and spiritual renewal. They provide a space where leaders can be human—flawed, tired, uncertain—without fear of judgment or exploitation.

Moreover, wise leaders create a culture in their organizations where vulnerability is not mistaken for weakness but rather recognized as courage. When leaders model appropriate transparency, they signal to their teams that trust is a two-way street. This doesn't mean oversharing or compromising professionalism; it means leading with authenticity, admitting mistakes, and demonstrating that strength and struggle can coexist.

Ultimately, leadership without trust is unsustainable. But leadership grounded in balanced, discerning trust—both given and received—creates an atmosphere where people thrive, teams unite, and vision becomes reality. Trust doesn't make leadership easier, but it makes it healthier, more enduring, and far more human.

Elijah Under the Broom Tree: Exhausted and Alone
The story of Elijah under the broom tree is one of the most profound and vulnerable moments in the Bible. It reveals the hidden struggles that often accompany the mantle of leadership, offering a glimpse into the emotional and spiritual toll that can come even after monumental victories. In 1 Kings 19, Elijah, the great prophet of Israel, stands at the edge of despair, far from the victorious hero who called down fire from heaven on Mount Carmel. The weight of leadership has crushed him, and his isolation and exhaustion are palpable.

A Victory Turned Hollow
Elijah had just experienced one of the most awe-inspiring moments in Israel's history—a showdown between the living God and the false god Baal on Mount Carmel. With unshakable boldness, Elijah challenged the 450 prophets of Baal to a public contest to determine once and for all who the true God was. The terms were simple: whichever deity answered by fire would be acknowledged as the One true God.

The prophets of Baal cried out to their god from morning till evening, cutting themselves and engaging in frenzied rituals, but their efforts ended in silence. Then Elijah, with calm confidence, rebuilt the altar of the Lord, drenched the offering in water three times, and prayed a simple but heartfelt prayer. In an instant, fire fell from heaven, consuming not only the offering but also the wood, the stones, and the water in the trench. It was a display of divine power that left no room for doubt. The people fell on their faces, crying out, "The Lord—He is God! The Lord—He is God!" (1 Kings 18:39). Revival had broken out. Idolatry had been exposed. Elijah had stood alone, yet he had seen the entire nation turn back to God. It was the kind of moment that any prophet would long for.

But just a chapter later, that victory feels painfully hollow.

Word of Elijah's triumph reaches Jezebel, the wicked queen whose heart burns with rage rather than repentance. Rather than being awestruck by God's power, she sends a chilling message to Elijah: *"May the gods deal with me, be it ever so severely, if by this time tomorrow I do not make your life like that of one of them."* (1 Kings 19:2). Suddenly, the bold prophet who had just stood fearless before a nation now flees into the wilderness, broken, exhausted, and suicidal. "I have had enough, Lord," Elijah says. "Take my life; I am no better than my ancestors" (1 Kings 19:4).

This dramatic shift from triumph to terror highlights a profound truth about human nature and spiritual leadership: even the strongest among us are not immune to despair. Elijah's story reveals the emotional toll of ministry and the vulnerability that often follows great spiritual victories. His fear was not merely physical—it was deeply emotional and spiritual. He was tired, disillusioned, and felt utterly alone.

How can such a high moment be followed so swiftly by such a low? The answer lies in the reality that spiritual warfare doesn't end with a victory—it often intensifies. Elijah expected change. He expected Jezebel to relent. He expected the revival at Mount Carmel to bring about permanent reform. But when that didn't happen, the weight of unmet expectations crushed him. What makes the story even more poignant is that Elijah didn't just fear Jezebel—he felt forgotten by God. He thought he was the only one left standing for righteousness. His sense of isolation magnified his despair.

But God, in His tender mercy, meets Elijah not with condemnation but with compassion. God sends an angel to feed him and let him rest. Then, God calls Elijah to Mount Horeb—not to rebuke him, but to reveal Himself. And in that encounter, God was not in the wind, the earthquake, or the fire, but in the gentle whisper. It was as though God was reminding Elijah: *"I am still here. You are not alone. And your purpose is not finished."*

Lessons from Elijah's Hollow Victory:
1. **Spiritual highs do not make us invincible.** Mountaintop

experiences are real, but they do not insulate us from discouragement. We must remain spiritually anchored after victories.
2. **Leadership can be lonely and emotionally draining.** Elijah's despair stemmed in part from feeling alone in his mission. God later reveals that 7,000 in Israel had not bowed to Baal. We may not always see the full impact of our obedience, but God does.
3. **God meets us in our weakness.** Elijah's story assures us that God does not discard us when we are broken. Instead, He nourishes us, restores us, and gently calls us forward.
4. **The battle doesn't end after one victory.** Just because God shows up in fire once doesn't mean the enemy gives up. Jezebel's threat reminds us that spiritual opposition persists—and we must persevere.

Elijah's story is not one of failure, but of God's faithfulness through frailty. It teaches us that even when our victories feel hollow, God still has a plan. The journey doesn't end in the wilderness. For every discouraged leader, tired believer, or weary soul—Elijah's story is a call to listen for the whisper of God's presence and keep moving forward.

The Wilderness of Isolation
In his fear and despair, Elijah retreats into the wilderness—a space that once symbolized divine revelation and intimacy with God. Now, it becomes a barren landscape mirroring the dryness within his own soul. The wilderness, often romanticized in biblical narratives as a place of transformation, here becomes a backdrop of intense emotional breakdown. Elijah, the mighty prophet who called down fire from heaven, who confronted kings and false

prophets, now finds himself slumped under a broom tree, overwhelmed and alone. This isn't just physical isolation—it's emotional and spiritual desolation.

Elijah's retreat is not simply about running from Jezebel's threats; it's a deeper escape from the crushing weight of expectations, opposition, and the silence that often follows miraculous moments. The highs of divine triumph are quickly followed by the lows of human frailty. Elijah collapses—not just in body, but in spirit. He is drained from the inside out. His desperate cry—"I have had enough, Lord. Take my life; I am no better than my ancestors"—reveals a profound internal struggle. He is not only tired; he is wrestling with his identity, his purpose, and his very worth.

This scene unveils a powerful truth: even those closest to God are not immune to despair. Elijah's words echo what many leaders, pastors, caregivers, parents, and individuals feel at some point in their journey—a deep weariness that questions, "Is it all worth it?" Leadership, especially spiritual leadership, can be a lonely path. After pouring out, guiding others, and standing in the gap, leaders can find themselves feeling empty, forgotten, and unappreciated.

There is a paradox here that should not be overlooked. Elijah had just been part of a visible, undeniable miracle—a mountaintop experience with the power of God on full display. Yet here he is, wishing for death. This sharp contrast reminds us that emotional and spiritual health doesn't automatically follow spiritual success. Miracles may stir the crowd, but they don't always refill the soul. Elijah's story reminds us that our humanity does not disappear in the face of divine assignments. In fact, the more significant the assignment, the more vulnerable we may become.

This wilderness moment speaks to all who have felt the crushing burden of expectations, those who have labored faithfully but now sit under their own "broom tree", wondering if they can go on. It's a call to recognize the silent suffering that often accompanies leadership and to make room for vulnerability. Elijah was not weak for feeling this way—he was human. And in this humanity, God did not rebuke him. Instead, God ministered to him through rest, food, and gentle presence.

In seasons of isolation, we must remember that God meets us there—not with condemnation, but with care. The wilderness may seem like a place of abandonment, but for Elijah, it became a place of restoration. And so, it can be for us. The same wilderness that exposed his weakness became the stage for God's gentle renewal.

The Burden of Leadership
Elijah's experience offers a profound window into the hidden struggles of leadership. On the surface, leadership is often portrayed as a noble calling—one marked by strength, wisdom, vision, and unshakable resolve. Leaders are seen as beacons of direction, confidence, and inspiration. They are the ones people look to in moments of crisis, the ones expected to have answers, take charge, and bear the load without complaint. But Elijah's story tears away that idealized veneer and reveals the raw, often lonely, inner reality of what it means to lead.

After a dramatic spiritual victory on Mount Carmel, where God answered his prayer with fire from heaven, Elijah should have been basking in triumph. But instead, he flees into the wilderness, terrified, discouraged, and ready to give up. He collapses under a broom tree and prays not for strength, not for guidance, and not for another miracle—but for his life to end. "Take my life; I am no better than my ancestors," he pleads (1 Kings 19:4). These are not the words of a weak or unfaithful man—they are the words of a burdened, exhausted, and deeply human leader who has reached the end of himself.

What's most striking about Elijah's plea is its honesty. He doesn't mask his fatigue with religious language. He doesn't pretend to be stronger than he is. He admits his despair. He's not just physically tired; he is emotionally drained and spiritually depleted. He feels isolated and ineffective, convinced that all his efforts have been in vain. This kind of transparency is rare among leaders, many of whom feel they must always appear composed and confident, even when they are unraveling inside.

Elijah's experience reflects a sobering truth: leadership can be a lonely and overwhelming path. The higher the position, the fewer people there are who truly understand the pressure. The decisions are heavier, the expectations greater, and the sacrifices steeper. Every move is scrutinized, every misstep magnified. And even when leaders succeed, the weight doesn't always lessen—it can increase. The mantle that once brought honor can begin to feel like a burden, a yoke that chases and weighs down the soul.

Many leaders find themselves in Elijah's shoes at some point—overworked, underappreciated, isolated, and on the verge of burnout. Yet, because of cultural or organizational expectations, they press on in silence, afraid to show weakness or admit discouragement. They lead on empty, hiding their wounds while continuing to pour into others.

But Elijah's story doesn't end under the broom tree. In response to his despair, God doesn't rebuke him or shame him. Instead, God meets Elijah in his brokenness. First, with rest and nourishment—through sleep and food brought by an angel. Then, with a gentle whisper, not a loud display of power. God reminds Elijah that he is not alone and that his journey is not yet over. He provides reassurance, direction, and companionship for the road ahead.

This part of the story carries a critical lesson: leaders need care too. They need rest, renewal, and the space to be vulnerable. They need to know that it's okay to be human, to cry out, and to receive help. Just as Elijah needed food, rest, and a divine reminder that he was not alone, so too do today's leaders need tangible and spiritual support.

Leadership is not about invincibility; it's about endurance. It's not about carrying everything alone—it's about knowing when to lean on others and when to be still and listen for the whisper of God. Elijah's story urges us to reimagine leadership not as a relentless climb to the top, but as a journey of faith marked by highs and lows, strength and weakness, victories and valleys.

Ultimately, Elijah's experience dignifies the pain that often comes with leadership. It gives voice to the silent suffering many carry and reminds us that even the greatest leaders are not immune to fear, fatigue, or failure. But it also offers hope—that in our lowest moments, God sees, God provides, and God speaks. And sometimes, the most powerful leadership comes not from standing tall, but from falling and letting God lift us up again.

The Divine Response: Grace in the Wilderness

In one of the most vulnerable moments of Elijah's life, we witness the heart of God in a deeply personal and compassionate way. After Elijah's dramatic confrontation on Mount Carmel, where fire fell from heaven and the prophets of Baal were defeated, we might expect his spirit to remain high. Yet, shortly afterward, we find him in a state of deep despair, running for his life, emotionally drained, and wishing for death. In this wilderness of fear, exhaustion, and isolation, God does not respond with condemnation or a call to toughen up. Instead, He responds with grace—gentle, thoughtful, and restorative.

Rather than scolding Elijah for his apparent lack of faith or resilience, God tends to his basic needs. He sends an angel to touch him, providing him with freshly baked bread and water, saying, "Get up and eat." But Elijah is still weary. He lies down again. And once more, God meets him in his need—not with impatience, but with another round of divine provision. Only after Elijah is physically nourished and rested does God speak to him again, offering direction and purpose.

This divine response is a profound lesson for all who lead—whether in ministry, family, or career. God shows us that the path to renewal does not begin with action, but with rest. Leaders, often driven by vision, responsibility, and the needs of others, can fall into the trap of believing that rest is indulgent or unproductive. But God flips that narrative. He demonstrates that rest is holy. Restoration is strategic. Renewal is a part of His divine plan for effective service.

When leaders find themselves in the wilderness—overwhelmed, burnt out, or feeling isolated—they must remember Elijah's story. God's grace meets us there. His voice often follows stillness, not noise. The strength to carry on is birthed not in striving but in surrender. Sometimes, the holiest thing a leader can do is step away, rest their body, quiet their soul, and let God minister to them.

God's response to Elijah also teaches us that our worth in His eyes is not tied to our performance, productivity, or public victories. Elijah had just accomplished one of the most dramatic miracles in Scripture, yet it's in his moment of exhaustion that we see God's intimate care most clearly. God didn't just want Elijah's ministry—He wanted Elijah's well-being. He valued the man more than the mission.

Ultimately, the wilderness becomes a place of encounter. It is there that Elijah hears the still small voice of God—not in the wind, not in the earthquake, not in the fire—but in the whisper. And so, it is with us. When we make room for rest and silence, we become receptive to the gentle voice of God that gives clarity, courage, and renewed purpose.

Let every leader take this to heart: You are not called to burn out for God but to burn brightly with His strength. The journey is long, and the calling is great, but divine grace will always provide what you need—sometimes in the form of bread, sometimes in the form of rest, and always in the form of His presence.

A Call to Renewed Purpose
After Elijah has rested and been nourished under God's care, we witness a profound shift in his journey—not just physically, but spiritually and emotionally. God does not allow Elijah to remain

in a state of hopelessness and isolation. Instead, He gently calls him out of the cave of despair and invites him to stand on the mountain in His presence. What follows is one of the most tender and transformative encounters in all of Scripture.

Elijah witnesses a mighty wind, a powerful earthquake, and a blazing fire—but God is not in any of them. These dramatic manifestations represent what one might expect of God's power, especially from the perspective of a prophet accustomed to dramatic signs like fire from heaven on Mount Carmel. Yet, God chooses to reveal Himself in a way Elijah did not anticipate—in a "still small voice" or a "gentle whisper." This is deeply symbolic. It shows that God's presence is not always found in the grand or sensational but often in the quiet, personal, and intimate moments. In Elijah's vulnerability, God meets him not with rebuke but with gentle reassurance.

This moment is a turning point. Elijah had felt alone, abandoned, and overwhelmed by the weight of his prophetic calling. He even asked God to take his life, believing his mission was over. But God, in His mercy, does not scold Elijah for his weariness. Instead, He renews Elijah's sense of purpose.

God gives Elijah a clear direction: he is to anoint Hazael as king over Aram, Jehu as king over Israel, and Elisha as his prophetic successor. This is not just a task list—it's a divine affirmation that Elijah's work is not finished. His role in shaping the future of God's people remains vital. Even in his lowest moment, God reaffirms that Elijah is still His chosen vessel.

Furthermore, God addresses Elijah's feeling of isolation by revealing that he is not alone—there are 7,000 in Israel who have not bowed to Baal or kissed him. This truth dismantles Elijah's belief that he is the last faithful servant left. Sometimes, in the depths of discouragement, we can feel utterly alone, but God reminds Elijah—and us—that He always preserves a faithful remnant, even when we cannot see them.

This encounter teaches us several powerful lessons:
- **God meets us in our weakness.** He understands our exhaustion and makes space for our recovery.
- **God speaks through the stillness.** In a noisy world, we must learn to listen for His gentle whisper.
- **God does not discard the weary.** Instead, He gives renewed vision, purpose, and direction.
- **God has a bigger picture.** What feels like the end to us may only be a chapter in God's unfolding plan.

In today's context, many leaders, ministers, and believers find themselves in moments like Elijah's—overwhelmed, discouraged, or ready to give up. But Elijah's story reminds us that God does not abandon us in our low points. Instead, He invites us into a deeper, quieter place where His presence brings clarity, healing, and new commissioning.

Your calling is not canceled because of your struggle. Your purpose is not lost in the storm. Like Elijah, God may be drawing you to a quiet place—not to punish you, but to restore you and re-ignite your mission with renewed purpose.

Elijah's Story as a Leadership Parable
The story of Elijah under the broom tree (1 Kings 19) stands as a powerful and timeless parable for leaders across every sphere— whether in ministry, business, family, or governance. It is a raw

and honest portrait of the emotional and spiritual toll leadership can take on even the most faithful and courageous individuals. Elijah, the prophet who had just called down fire from heaven and boldly confronted the prophets of Baal, finds himself running for his life, filled with fear, despair, and exhaustion. He retreats into the wilderness, sits under a broom tree, and cries out, "It is enough; now, O Lord, take away my life…"

This moment of collapse is not just a historical account; it is a mirror held up to the soul of every leader who has ever felt overwhelmed by the demands of their calling. Elijah had reached his limit—not because he was weak, but because he was human. And therein lies the first lesson: **leadership does not exempt one from weariness.**

1. Leadership is Often Lonely
Elijah had just witnessed a great victory on Mount Carmel, but it did not shield him from fear and loneliness. Leadership can be incredibly isolating. When you lead, you often carry burdens others do not see. Expectations are high, pressure is constant, and failure feels like it is not an option. Elijah ran into the wilderness not just to escape danger but to escape the crushing solitude of leadership without immediate support.

For modern leaders, this part of Elijah's journey reminds us of the importance of **community and connection**. We are not called to lead alone. God never intended for the weight of leadership to rest on one set of shoulders. Even the strongest need others to walk alongside them.

2. Burnout is Real—Even for the God-Ordained
Elijah's physical, emotional, and spiritual exhaustion is a vivid

picture of burnout. He was not running from failure; he was running after success. The emotional high of victory was followed by a steep emotional crash. His body was drained, his soul was disillusioned, and his perspective became distorted—he believed he was the only one left serving God.

This teaches us that **success does not insulate us from burnout**. Leaders must be vigilant, not only in managing tasks and responsibilities but also in tending to their inner world. Rest is not a luxury—it is a necessity. Even Jesus withdrew to quiet places to pray and rest. God's response to Elijah was not a lecture or rebuke, but tender care. He allowed Elijah to sleep, sent an angel to feed him, and gave him space to recover.

3. God Meets Us in Our Low Places

Perhaps the most beautiful part of Elijah's story is how God responded to his brokenness. There was no condemnation, no shame, no harsh rebuke—only grace. God met Elijah right where he was: tired, afraid, and disillusioned. He provided food, rest, and ultimately, direction.

This is a vital reminder for leaders: **God does not despise your humanity**. He understands your fears and sees your tears. When you feel like giving up, God steps in not to replace you, but to restore you. He gently reminded Elijah that he was not alone—there were still 7,000 who had not bowed to Baal. Elijah's perspective was limited by his pain, but God saw the full picture.

4. Rest Precedes Revelation

It was not in Elijah's striving but in his stillness that he encountered the voice of God. After rest and nourishment, Elijah was taken to Mount Horeb. There, in a cave, God revealed

Himself—not in the wind, or the earthquake, or the fire—but in a **gentle whisper**. This divine whisper cut through Elijah's fear and renewed his sense of purpose.

For today's leaders, the lesson is profound: **we often hear God best when we slow down**. Busyness can drown out the voice of God. But in solitude, in silence, and after surrender, we find clarity. God used that moment to recommission Elijah—to remind him of his calling and to send him back with renewed strength.

5. Your Calling Continues, Even After Collapse

Elijah's story under the broom tree could have ended as a tragic tale of burnout and withdrawal. But it didn't. It became the turning point in his ministry. After being refreshed, Elijah anointed Elisha as his successor, confronted kings, and continued his prophetic work until the very end. His story did not stop in the wilderness, it was *redirected*.

For every leader who feels like quitting, Elijah's story is a reminder that **failure or fatigue does not disqualify you**. God still has work for you to do. He does not define you by your moment of weakness but by His purpose for your life. What feels like the end may actually be the beginning of a more mature, more fruitful, and more dependent phase of your leadership journey.

The Leadership Legacy of Elijah

Elijah's broom tree experience offers a holistic leadership parable: that success and weariness can coexist, that leaders are not immune to despair, and that God's grace is sufficient to restore what exhaustion has drained. For every leader who has ever felt alone, discouraged, or on the brink of giving up—Elijah's story is a sacred encouragement: **you are not forgotten, you are not alone, and you are not finished.**

God still speaks. He still restores. And like Elijah, you too can rise from the wilderness—renewed, redirected, and ready to continue the journey ahead.

The Path to Restoration
In the story of Elijah, we witness a powerful narrative of God's compassion and the importance of rest and renewal for those in leadership. Elijah, a prophet of God, found himself overwhelmed, running in fear, exhausted, and emotionally drained after a series of intense battles and spiritual warfare. His encounter with the angel, who provided him with food, water, and the opportunity to sleep, offers deep insights into how leaders can navigate their own moments of despair and exhaustion.

God did not leave Elijah in his despair. Instead, He met him with compassion and practical care. The angel touched him, providing sustenance and rest before addressing any spiritual needs. This is a profound lesson for leaders: restoration begins not in striving, but in receiving. God's intervention in Elijah's life was not only about spiritual revival but also about tending to his physical needs first. The angel knew that Elijah needed rest, sustenance, and time to heal before he could carry on with the work ahead.

The Importance of Rest and Reflection
In our fast-paced, achievement-driven world, leadership is often equated with constant motion, unbroken productivity, and

emotional resilience. Society pressures leaders to maintain a facade of invincibility, pushing them to keep going no matter what the cost. However, true leadership is not defined by relentless striving but by wisdom, the kind of wisdom that discerns when to pause, when to retreat, and when to allow room for rest and reflection.

Rest is not a luxury or an afterthought; it is a divine principle woven into the fabric of creation. From the beginning, God modeled rest by ceasing from His work on the seventh day, not because He was tired, but to establish a rhythm for humanity—a pattern of work and rest that honors both productivity and restoration. Leaders who ignore this rhythm do so at their peril, often finding themselves burned out, depleted, and disconnected from their purpose.

The story of the prophet Elijah offers a powerful reminder of this truth. After his dramatic confrontation with the prophets of Baal and a period of intense spiritual warfare, Elijah found himself overwhelmed, exhausted, and afraid. He fled into the wilderness, praying that he might die. But instead of rebuking him, God responded with compassion. He provided food, water, and, most importantly, the space to rest. Elijah was told to sleep—and then sleep again—before receiving further instructions. This moment illustrates that rest is not a sign of weakness; it is a sign of wisdom and divine care. Before Elijah could receive the next phase of his assignment, he first had to be restored.

Leaders today must adopt this same posture of humility. Recognizing our limits is not a failure in leadership; it is foundational to healthy, sustainable influence. True restoration begins when we are honest about our fatigue, our doubts, and our need for renewal. In ministry, business, family, or community leadership, pouring out constantly without being filled leads to spiritual dryness and emotional burnout. The act of pausing—whether through a sabbath, a retreat, or moments of solitude—is not selfish; it is sacred.

Jesus Himself exemplified this balance. Amid the demands of His public ministry, He frequently withdrew to solitary places to pray, rest, and reconnect with the Father. If the Son of God deemed it necessary to step away from the crowd and replenish His soul, how much more should we? These moments of quiet are not wasted time; they are sacred encounters where clarity is restored, strength is renewed, and vision is refreshed.

Reflection, too, plays a crucial role in this process. In stillness, we gain perspective. We learn to see beyond the urgent and into the eternal. It is in moments of quiet reflection that we realign with God's voice, rediscover our "why," and evaluate whether we are leading from a place of calling or compulsion. Rest without reflection can lead to stagnation, but when the two are paired, they become powerful tools of transformation.

To lead well, one must live well—and living well includes honoring the rhythms of rest God designed for us. Let us not glorify busyness or wear exhaustion as a badge of honor. Instead, may we embrace rest as a form of worship, a declaration that we trust God to sustain the work while we lie still. In doing so, we not only preserve our health and clarity—we also model a healthier, more faithful way of leading for those who follow us.

God's Provision in Times of Despair

One of the most powerful moments in the life of the prophet Elijah is not found in his confrontation with the prophets of Baal or in the miracles he performed, but in the quiet, intimate moment of his despair. After a major spiritual victory on Mount Carmel, Elijah fled into the wilderness, overwhelmed by fear, loneliness, and exhaustion. He reached a breaking point and cried out to God, saying, *"I have had enough, Lord. Take my life"* (1 Kings 19:4). Elijah, a bold prophet, became a broken man—but in this place of deep vulnerability, God began the work of restoration.

The second key aspect of Elijah's restoration was *God's provision*. What is striking in this passage is how God responded to Elijah's despair—not with rebuke, but with compassion. God did not scold Elijah for being fearful or weary. He did not demand that Elijah pull himself together or question his faith. Instead, God met Elijah in his lowest moment and gave him exactly what he needed: rest, food, water, and time.

Physical Provision First, Then Spiritual Renewal

Before addressing Elijah's spiritual condition, God dealt with his physical needs. An angel touched Elijah and said, *"Get up and eat."* He looked around, and there by his head was a cake of bread baked over hot coals and a jar of water (1 Kings 19:5-6). Elijah ate and lay down again. This cycle repeated, and only after Elijah had been nourished and strengthened was he ready to continue the journey toward Horeb, the mountain of God.

This sequence is deeply instructive. God understands that we are holistic beings—body, soul, and spirit. In times of despair, sometimes what we need first is not a sermon, but sleep. Not a solution, but sustenance. The Lord tends to our frailty with gentleness. This is a vital lesson for leaders who often feel the pressure to always be strong, always be available, always keep going. God's provision reminds us that rest is not laziness, and receiving help is not weakness.

God's Presence Is the Ultimate Provision
After Elijah was physically strengthened, God drew him into a deeper place of spiritual restoration. On Mount Horeb, God revealed Himself—not in the wind, earthquake, or fire, but in a gentle whisper (1 Kings 19:11-12). This whisper symbolized the intimate, sustaining presence of God. Elijah didn't just need power—he needed presence. He didn't need a dramatic sign—he needed divine reassurance.

This speaks volumes to anyone leading through seasons of discouragement, burnout, or spiritual dryness. God's provision is not always flashy. It often comes in quiet, consistent ways—through His Word, through worship, through fellowship, and through stillness. In these sacred moments, God renews our purpose, realigns our perspective, and reminds us that we are never alone.

Our Strength Comes from God, Not Ourselves
Elijah continued his mission, but not in his own strength. His restoration was a result of receiving from God. This underscores a profound truth for all leaders: *while we are called to lead and serve, our strength does not come from our own abilities but from the grace and strength that God provides*. The Apostle Paul echoed this when he said, *"But he said to me, 'My grace is sufficient for you, for my power is made perfect in weakness.'"* (2 Corinthians 12:9).

In moments of despair or exhaustion, we must resist the cultural lie that says, "Just push through." Instead, we are invited to *receive*—to rest in the promises of God, to rely on His strength, and to be honest about our limitations. True restoration begins when we humble ourselves enough to admit that we need help.

Receiving from God Requires Humility

In a world that celebrates self-sufficiency and rewards relentless striving, it can feel counterintuitive to stop and admit, *"I can't do this on my own."* Yet, the posture that opens the floodgates of heaven's provision is not one of prideful determination, but of humility. Often, the path to healing and restoration is not paved with grand gestures or dramatic breakthroughs, but with quiet surrender and honest vulnerability.

It takes humility to pause when everyone expects you to keep going. It takes humility to raise your hand and say, *"I need help."* It takes humility to ask for prayer, to seek wise counsel, to step away from responsibilities for a season, or even to simply say, *"I'm not okay."* But these seemingly small and human moments are the exact places where God meets us with divine grace.

Throughout Scripture, God consistently lifts the humble and resists the proud. Why? Because humility makes space for God. When we release our grip on control, perfectionism, and appearances, we make room for Him to move, to comfort, to restore, and to provide. His provision comes in many forms, sometimes through a Scripture that speaks directly to our pain, other times through a much-needed sabbatical that brings clarity and renewal, or through the love of a community that refuses to let us fall through the cracks. God's provision is always timely, always sufficient, and always bathed in love.

Elijah's story is a powerful reminder. After his dramatic confrontation with the prophets of Baal, we find him not rejoicing in victory, but running into the wilderness, overwhelmed and despairing. It's there—in the dry, silent, lonely place—that God ministers to him. Not with another spectacle, but with simple acts of care: a warm meal, gentle sleep, and a quiet whisper. God didn't scold Elijah for being exhausted. He didn't shame him for being afraid. Instead, He met Elijah right where he was and gave him exactly what he needed.

This is who our God is—not only the God of miracles and mountaintops, but the God of valleys and shadows. He doesn't restore us by demanding more from us; He restores us by *giving* what we lack. He supplies strength when we're weak, peace when we're anxious, direction when we're lost, and love when we feel unworthy.

As leaders, servants, parents, pastors, or mentors, we must remember this: we are not called to serve out of depletion, but out of the *overflow* of God's grace. Ministry, leadership, and life are not sustainable without continual receiving. We cannot pour out if we are not being filled. The lie of constant productivity must be replaced with the truth of divine rhythm—*work and rest, give and receive, lead and be led.*

To receive from God is not a sign of failure; it is a mark of spiritual maturity. It's how we stay rooted. It's how we keep our hearts soft. And it's how we avoid burnout and bitterness.

So, in your moments of despair, fatigue, or discouragement, don't run from God—run *to* Him. Cry if you must. Sit in silence. Reach out to others. Take a break. Do whatever humility requires, because in that space, God draws near. He is the God who sees. The God who understands. And the God who always provides.

Let humility lead you back to the arms of the Father. Let surrender make way for supernatural strength. And let God remind you that you don't have to hold everything together—He already is.

The Loneliness of Leadership
One of the most poignant and relatable themes in Elijah's journey is the profound loneliness that can accompany leadership. After the dramatic showdown on Mount Carmel, where God demonstrated His power through Elijah in front of the prophets of Baal, one might expect Elijah to be filled with confidence and spiritual momentum. Yet, immediately afterward, he finds himself running for his life, driven by fear of Queen Jezebel's threat. Isolated in the wilderness, Elijah reaches a breaking point. He collapses under a broom tree and pleads with God to end his life, saying, *"I have had enough, Lord… I am no better than my ancestors"* (1 Kings 19:4). These are not the words of a man who is weak, but of a man who is weary—a man burdened by the weight of leadership and the sting of perceived failure and solitude.

This moment exposes a harsh truth: leadership, even when done faithfully, can feel incredibly lonely.

For many leaders, whether in ministry, business, family, or community, the loneliness Elijah experienced is all too familiar. Carrying the responsibility for others, making decisions that may not always be understood or appreciated, and enduring seasons of apparent fruitlessness can create an emotional and spiritual wilderness. Leaders often put on a brave face, expected to be pillars of strength and clarity, yet inside they may battle discouragement, doubt, and a longing for companionship and understanding.

Elijah's assumption that he was the only faithful servant left ("I alone am left...") mirrors the internal voices leaders often hear in times of exhaustion: *"No one gets it." "I'm all alone." "This burden is mine to carry."* But God, in His compassion, responds not with rebuke, but with gentleness. He meets Elijah in the wilderness—not in thunder or earthquake, but in a *gentle whisper*. In that still, small voice, God speaks life back into His servant. He provides rest, nourishment, and most importantly, perspective. Elijah was not alone; God had preserved seven thousand in Israel who had not bowed to Baal.

This revelation is crucial: **leaders are rarely as alone as they feel.** God is always at work behind the scenes, and He often surrounds His servants with more support than they realize. But in order to see it, leaders must be still long enough to hear God's whisper above the noise of fear and fatigue.

Elijah's story also teaches that divine restoration comes in stages—rest, food, sleep, presence, and purpose. God didn't just speak to Elijah; He nourished him. He allowed him to rest, and then He gave him new instructions, a renewed sense of mission. Leadership might bring moments of wilderness, but God never leaves His leaders to wither there. He restores and reassigns.

For leaders today, this offers deep encouragement:
- **Loneliness is real, but it is not final.** It's a season, not a

sentence.

- **God sees you even when others don't.** Your labor, your tears, your silent prayers are known to Him.
- **You need rest and replenishment.** Burnout is not a badge of honor. Even the strongest leaders need space to recover.
- **You are not alone.** God often has "seven thousand others" you may not yet see—mentors, peers, encouragers, or silent intercessors placed around you for your strengthening.
- **Your calling still stands.** Even after failure, fear, or fatigue, God is not done with you. He will redirect and reignite your purpose.

In a world that often glorifies productivity over presence, leaders must learn to listen for the whisper of God, especially in the wilderness. It is there that God reminds us: *You are mine. You are not alone. Rise again—I still have work for you to do.*

Leaning into God's Grace

The restoration of Elijah offers a profound and timeless invitation to every leader: **lean into God's grace.** Leadership, though a noble calling, often comes with weighty expectations, emotional demands, and spiritual warfare. It can feel lonely, exhausting, and even disillusioning, especially when the results of one's labor seem invisible or met with resistance. Elijah, the mighty prophet who once called down fire from heaven, found himself fleeing in fear, depleted and discouraged. Yet, it was in that place of brokenness that God met him—not with rebuke, but with grace.

Elijah's encounter with God in 1 Kings 19 reminds us that **leadership was never meant to be sustained by human strength alone.** When Elijah collapsed under a broom tree, praying that he might die, God did not shame him for his despair.

Instead, He sent an angel to minister to him—with food, water, and rest. This act of divine compassion is a powerful reminder that God cares not just about our performance but about our person—our bodies, our emotions, and our souls.

Leadership can become a heavy burden when we assume it must be carried without pause. But the truth is, **leaders are called to serve from a place of divine dependence, not self-sufficiency.** We are not machines; we are vessels—fragile, yes, but also capable of being filled with God's strength. Leaning into grace means recognizing that we are not limitless. It means acknowledging our humanity, our need for rest, and our deep dependence on God's sustaining power.

Elijah's restoration did not come from a dramatic sign or a miraculous intervention—it came through **stillness, gentleness, and presence.** In the cave, God spoke not through the wind, earthquake, or fire, but through a still, small voice. This teaches us that **God often meets us in the quiet**, not the chaos. And sometimes, the most spiritual thing a leader can do is to pause, rest, and listen.

True leadership is not about carrying the mantle alone. It is about **knowing when to lay our burdens down at the feet of Jesus**, who says, *"Come to me, all you who are weary and burdened, and I will give you rest"* (Matthew 11:28). It is about admitting, like Elijah, that we have limits—and trusting that God will meet us there, not with condemnation, but with comfort and provision.

To lean into God's grace is to:
- Embrace **vulnerability**, admitting when we are tired or overwhelmed.

- Prioritize **spiritual rhythms**—prayer, rest, solitude, and scripture.
- Allow others to help carry the load, knowing that leadership is not a solo calling.
- Trust that **God is working even when we feel like we're failing.**
- Believe that **rest is not weakness, but wisdom.**

In the same way that God sent Elijah an angel, He sends us His Spirit, His Word, and sometimes, His people, to lift us up when we can no longer go on. Let us, as leaders, learn from Elijah—not only how to call down fire, but how to **retreat into grace** when the fire fades. For it is in God's presence that we find the strength to rise again and continue the journey—not alone but empowered by His mercy and love.

A Call to Prioritize Well-Being
Elijah's story is more than an account of a weary prophet; it is a divine invitation—a call for leaders to prioritize their well-being, both physically and spiritually. After one of the most dramatic spiritual victories on Mount Carmel, Elijah found himself in a place of deep despair, isolation, and exhaustion. His experience reminds us that even the strongest among us are vulnerable to fatigue, discouragement, and emotional collapse. Leadership does not exempt one from human frailty; rather, it often magnifies the weight of responsibility, making self-care not a luxury but a necessity.

Restoration is a journey, not a Moment. Elijah's journey from burnout to restoration was not instantaneous. It was marked by God's tender intervention—through rest, nourishment, solitude, and finally, a gentle whisper. This reminds us that restoration is not a one-time event, but an ongoing process that requires intentional reflection, consistent care, and unwavering reliance on God. Leaders must learn to recognize the signs of depletion and be willing to pause. This pause is not an admission of weakness but a courageous act of humility—acknowledging one's limitations and inviting God's strength into our weakness.

The Myth of the Invincible Leader
In a culture that celebrates hustle, glorifies overwork, and often equates productivity with worth, Elijah's encounter with God offers a much-needed countercultural message. True leadership is not defined by relentless activity or visible achievements, but by an inner strength that comes from rest, renewal, and the recognition of God's provision. Elijah needed rest before he received further instructions. He needed to be reminded that he was not alone, and that God still had a plan.

Likewise, leaders today must learn to rest not just to recharge, but to realign—with purpose, with calling, and most importantly, with the voice of God. Leadership that is disconnected from divine strength is destined to collapse under the weight of expectations.

Leadership Requires Community
One of the most powerful truths from Elijah's story is that the road of leadership was never meant to be walked alone. God reminded Elijah that he was not the only faithful one left—there were 7,000 others who had not bowed to Baal. This revelation shattered Elijah's sense of isolation and reinforced the necessity of community. Today's leaders must resist the temptation of

isolation and instead pursue healthy relationships—with mentors, peers, and spiritual support systems.

Burnout thrives in silence, secrecy, and shame. Healing, on the other hand, blossoms in environments of openness, accountability, and shared burdens. Leadership is not about carrying everything alone, but about walking in step with God and in connection with others.

The First Step: Lean into Grace
True restoration doesn't begin with a to-do list—it begins with grace. It's not about proving ourselves or performing harder. It starts when we acknowledge our humanity, our limitations, and our deep need for the One who never tires, never burns out, and never abandons us in our weakness. Restoration begins the moment we stop striving and start surrendering.

To *lean into grace* is to turn away from the false belief that strength is measured by endless productivity or constant visibility. It is to embrace the quiet truth that God loves us not because of what we do, but because of who He is. Grace invites us to come undone in His presence—not to be fixed quickly, but to be known fully.

This posture of surrender often requires intentional pauses: stepping away from platforms, demands, and noise. It may look like physical rest—taking a sabbath, saying no, or turning off our phones. It may involve spiritual retreat—immersing ourselves in Scripture, prayer, and solitude to re-center our hearts. For others, it may require professional help, such as counseling, to process pain, trauma, or burnout. Whatever the form, these rhythms are not indulgences; they are acts of obedience and trust.

Leaders, in particular, must guard their inner world. Not just for their own wellbeing, but for the sake of those they influence. When a leader is weary, disconnected, or spiritually dry, it affects entire communities. A healthy leader nurtures healthy people. But that health is not sustained by grit; it is sustained by grace.

Elijah's journey is a poignant example. After a stunning spiritual victory on Mount Carmel, he crashed into despair. He was exhausted, fearful, and ready to give up. But God didn't rebuke Elijah for his weakness. Instead, He fed him, let him rest, and eventually met him—not in the spectacle of the wind, earthquake, or fire, but in a *gentle whisper*. That whisper came in stillness—after the noise had died down.

And so, it is with us. Restoration often begins in the silence we fear but desperately need. It begins in the holy pause, where we hear the whisper of God saying, "You are not alone. You are still Mine."

So, before you run harder, lead stronger, or try to push through the pain—stop. Breathe. Lean into grace. Let yourself be held, healed, and humbled in the arms of the One who restores souls.

Because the first step forward... is always stillness.

A Restoration Journey for Every Leader
Leadership often carries the weight of unspoken expectations, strength without weakness, wisdom without error, consistency without fatigue. But the truth is, even the most faithful leaders reach moments when their inner strength wanes, their vision blurs, and their spirits ache for rest. The journey of restoration is not a detour from leadership; it is a necessary part of it. It is not

defined by titles, applause, or accomplishments. Rather, it is marked by the humility to pause, the courage to rest, and the faith to seek God in the quiet places.

Restoration begins when a leader recognizes that they cannot pour from an empty vessel. Just as God met Elijah under the broom tree—not with condemnation, but with care—He meets every leader who dares to be vulnerable. Elijah had just called down fire from heaven, yet he collapsed in despair, crying, "I have had enough, Lord." In that moment, God didn't demand more work from him. Instead, He offered rest, sustenance, and His gentle presence. This divine encounter reminds us that God does not discard weary leaders; He revives them.

Leadership is not about projecting invincibility. It is about learning to lead from a place of dependence on God's strength, not one's own. It is about understanding that being overwhelmed does not make you unworthy; it makes you human. And in our humanity, God's grace shines the brightest.

To walk the restoration journey, a leader must do three things:
1. **Pause Intentionally** – Take deliberate steps to stop and evaluate. Rest is not laziness; it is a spiritual discipline. In quietness and stillness, God speaks the loudest. Pausing allows the soul to catch up with the pace of leadership.
2. **Seek God Deeply** – Restoration is not found in distractions, achievements, or performance. It is found in the secret place—in prayer, in worship, and in God's Word. When leaders return to the well of His presence, they find living water that truly refreshes.
3. **Receive Without Earning** – Many leaders struggle to rest because they feel guilty when they are not producing. But

God's restoration is a gift, not a reward. He prepares a table before you, not because you've earned it, but because you're His child.

Fatigue, fear, and loneliness are not signs of failure; they are signals that it's time to draw closer to the Source of strength. God's presence is not reserved for perfect leaders; it is extended to honest ones. He walks with those who admit, "I can't do this on my own anymore."

Every leader, no matter how seasoned or anointed, needs moments of sacred restoration. In those moments, God does not push us forward in our brokenness; He heals us, strengthens us, and walks beside us. The journey is not over. The calling has not been revoked. The God who called you still stands by you, offering the rest you didn't know you needed and the strength you thought was gone.

So, pause. Rest. Breathe. Trust. The God who restored Elijah is the same God who will restore you.

PART TWO: BLEEDING TYPES – DIFFERENT WOUNDS

CHAPTER 4
Emotional Bleeding

Emotional bleeding refers to the deep, internal wounds caused by repeated emotional strain, betrayal, neglect, or overwhelming responsibility. Unlike physical wounds, emotional bleeding isn't always visible to others, but its effects can be just as debilitating, impacting one's mental health, relationships, productivity, and spiritual well-being. The following are some of the major sources of emotional bleeding:

1. Betrayal by Close Allies.

Betrayal is painful, but betrayal by someone we considered a close ally is a wound like no other. It is not just the action of being wronged that hurts—it's the shock, the disbelief, and the heartbreak of realizing that someone we once held close, someone we loved, confided in, and depended on, could so easily turn against us. Whether it's a trusted friend spreading rumors, a family member choosing sides during conflict, or a colleague sabotaging us for personal gain, the emotional injury runs deep.

These are not strangers or acquaintances. These are individuals we allowed into the sacred spaces of our hearts. We gave them access to our vulnerabilities, our dreams, our fears, our joys. That level of closeness makes the betrayal feel like a violation of our soul.

The fallout of such betrayal can be devastating:

- **A Deep Sense of Isolation:** The pain of betrayal often drives us into emotional isolation. We retreat into ourselves, feeling that no one can truly be trusted. The very people we once leaned on are now the ones we've learned to fear, making it difficult to open up again.
- **Difficulty Trusting Others Again:** When trust is shattered by someone close, rebuilding it with others feels almost impossible. Even new and innocent relationships are viewed with suspicion. Every compliment is questioned, every gesture dissected for hidden motives.
- **Internal Questions and Self-Blame:** Victims of betrayal often turn inward, haunted by self-doubt. Questions like "Why me?", "Was I not good enough?" or "What did I do to deserve this?" became constant companions. We replay events, overanalyze words, and struggle to find what we could have done differently.
- **Cynicism and Emotional Detachment:** To avoid future pain, many build emotional walls so high that genuine connections become nearly impossible. Love is approached with caution. Friendships are kept at arm's length. Vulnerability is seen as a threat rather than a gift.

Why does it hurt so much?

Betrayal from a close ally isn't just about the loss of a relationship; it's about the loss of identity. We often define ourselves through the roles we play in others' lives: the loyal friend, the supportive sibling, the dependable coworker. When someone we served in love and loyalty turns around and wounds us, it shakes the foundation of who we thought we were.

The experience can feel like being emotionally ambushed. You thought you were safe, only to discover you were vulnerable in the worst way. This emotional bleeding can lead to feelings of worthlessness, abandonment, and deep sadness. In extreme cases, it can trigger depression, anxiety, and long-term emotional trauma.

Healing from Betrayal
Recovery is not easy, but it is possible. It begins by acknowledging the pain without minimizing it. Permit yourself to grieve—not just the betrayal, but the loss of what you thought the relationship was. Seek support from people who are genuinely safe and caring. Therapy, prayer, journaling, or talking with a trusted mentor can also help process the hurt.

Most importantly, know that betrayal is a reflection of the betrayer, not your worth. People hurt others from a place of brokenness, envy, insecurity, or selfishness. Their choice to betray says more about their character than it ever does about yours.

Healing does not mean forgetting or reconciling. It means reclaiming your peace, restoring your sense of identity, and refusing to let someone else's betrayal define your future.

Timothy Abandoned by Leaders in the Church
Timothy, a young and faithful companion of the Apostle Paul, was no stranger to the harsh realities of ministry. Despite his spiritual maturity, loyalty, and unwavering dedication to the work of God, there were moments when he faced deep discouragement—not just from external opposition, but from within the very community he served: the church.

Paul's second letter to Timothy reveals the emotional weight of abandonment, particularly in **2 Timothy 1:15**, where Paul writes, "You know that everyone in the province of Asia has deserted me, including Phygelus and Hermogenes." This statement doesn't exclude Timothy from the fallout. As Paul's closest disciple and representative, Timothy would have felt the sting of that desertion too—either directly through personal rejection or indirectly through the cold winds of discouragement as ministry companions turned away.

The Pain of Being Left Alone
Timothy, though deeply respected by Paul, had to carry the burden of seeing others walk away from the faith or from the responsibilities of leadership. Leaders who once served with passion became weary, distracted, or disloyal. This would have been disheartening for a young minister trying to remain faithful. The emotional strain of being surrounded by instability in leadership can make one feel isolated, even in the midst of spiritual service.

Leadership Abandonment is Not New
Church leaders stepping away or withdrawing their support is not a modern problem—it has biblical roots. Timothy's experience reminds us that not everyone who starts strong in ministry finishes well. Some fall into error, others into compromise, and some simply grow cold or fearful. In **2 Timothy 4:10**, Paul laments that "Demas, having loved this present world, has deserted me." Such desertions would have affected the morale of Timothy and others trying to stay the course.

Emotional and Spiritual Strain
Being abandoned by leaders isn't just a blow to organizational strength; it wounds the soul. Timothy, who struggled with timidity and physical weakness (1 Timothy 5:23), likely wrestled with fear, anxiety, and moments of self-doubt. When those you look up to walk away or disappoint you, it shakes your confidence and can lead to deep discouragement.

The Call to Stand Firm Despite Abandonment
Paul repeatedly encouraged Timothy to stay strong, hold on to sound doctrine, and keep his faith alive even when others failed him. **2 Timothy 1:6-7** says, "Fan into flame the gift of God… for the Spirit God gave us does not make us timid, but gives us power, love and self-discipline." This shows Paul knew Timothy would need inner strength when outward support failed. The call was to stand firm, not because of the consistency of others, but because of the unchanging faithfulness of God.

God's Faithfulness in the Midst of Human Failure
Though church leaders may abandon, God never does. Paul tells Timothy in **2 Timothy 4:16-17**, "At my first defense, no one came to my support, but everyone deserted me. But the Lord stood at my side and gave me strength…" This truth was just as much for Timothy as it was for Paul. God's presence fills the void left by human disappointment.

Encouragement for Today's Leaders
If you, like Timothy, have experienced abandonment by leaders, know that you're not alone. Even faithful servants of God face betrayal, silence, and absence from those who once stood with them. But your calling is not dependent on the consistency of

others—it is anchored in the faithfulness of God. Keep serving. Keep believing. And like Timothy, fan into flame the gift God has placed within you.

2. Leadership Burnout

Leadership is a noble calling. It demands courage, vision, sacrifice, and resilience. Whether you're leading in ministry, business, family, or community, stepping into a leadership role often means stepping into the fire. The constant need to be strong for others, to make tough decisions, to mediate conflicts, and to inspire those around you can gradually take a toll.

The truth is, leadership can be exhausting—and lonely.

Many leaders are celebrated for their results but seldom understood in their pain. They give without expecting anything in return, pour themselves out daily while rarely being filled, and carry burdens that are invisible to those they lead. In the eyes of others, they are strong, capable, and steady. But beneath the surface, they may be tired, depleted, and silently struggling.

Symptoms of Leadership Burnout
Burnout doesn't always happen overnight. It often creeps in slowly, silently, until it becomes a crippling force. Warning signs include:

- **Emotional exhaustion and numbness** – You're no longer moved by what used to inspire you. Joy becomes a memory.
- **Irritability or frequent emotional breakdowns** – You react more strongly to minor issues, or break down in private moments, feeling overwhelmed by the weight you carry.

- **Feeling unappreciated or taken for granted** – You start to wonder if your sacrifices even matter or if anyone truly sees your efforts.
- **Loss of passion or purpose** – That thing you once loved doing now feels like a chore. You begin to question why you started in the first place.
- **Physical symptoms** – Fatigue, insomnia, anxiety, frequent illness, and unexplained aches often accompany emotional and mental overload.

The Silent Danger
When a leader continues to pour while bleeding emotionally, they risk not just burnout, but breakdown. Their health begins to crumble, their spiritual life suffers, and their relationships deteriorate. They may still appear functional on the outside, but inside, they are battling discouragement, disillusionment, and despair.

Worse still, when burnout is ignored, it can lead to compromised integrity. A weary leader is more vulnerable to temptation, poor judgment, and even moral failure—not because they are bad people, but because they are simply drained. When the well runs dry, even good intentions can no longer sustain wise leadership.

Leadership without replenishment is emotional suicide. You can't pour from an empty vessel.

The Call to Replenish
If you are a leader, hear this: **You are not a machine. You are a human being—spirit, soul, and body.** You are allowed to rest. You are allowed to say no. You are allowed to ask for help. You are not called to die while trying to keep everyone else alive.

Replenishment is not a luxury; it's a necessity. Even Jesus, the perfect leader, often withdrew from the crowds to rest, pray, and reconnect with the Father (Luke 5:16). If the Son of God needed moments of solitude and spiritual refueling, how much more do we?

Here are a few ways to resist and recover from burnout:

- **Establish boundaries** – Learn to say no. Every open door is not a divine assignment.
- **Delegate and develop others** – You're not called to do everything. Empower others to lead.
- **Create space for solitude and reflection** – Rest is holy. Make time to be quiet and reconnect with your purpose.
- **Invest in relationships that give back** – Not every connection should be a one-way street. Surround yourself with people who replenish your soul.
- **Prioritize spiritual disciplines** – Prayer, worship, and the Word of God are not optional for the leader—they are lifelines.
- **Seek wise counsel** – A coach, mentor, or counselor can help you process your weariness and regain clarity.

Leadership is not about being superhuman; it's about being surrendered. God never called you to carry what only He can sustain. The same God who called you to lead also cares deeply about your soul.

Take off the cape. You were never called to save the world—Jesus already did that. You were called to serve faithfully, not to run yourself into the ground.

You can lead well *and* live well. But only if you allow yourself to pause, breathe, receive, and rest. Healing begins where honesty is embraced. So, if you're tired, say it. If you're weak, acknowledge it. And let God, your true Source, restore what life and leadership have drained.

3. Emotional Neglect or Overload

Emotional neglect happens when your emotional needs are **consistently ignored, minimized, or dismissed** by those who are supposed to care. This can come from a spouse who is physically present but emotionally distant, from family members who expect your support but never offer theirs in return, or even from a spiritual community that praises your service while overlooking your pain.

You might be the one who shows up for everyone, always listening, encouraging, comforting—yet when you need someone to lean on, **there's no one there**. You feel invisible, unheard, and forgotten. It's not that people are overtly cruel; it's that they fail to *see you*.

Neglect says: "Your needs don't matter."

And over time, you begin to believe it.

What is Emotional Overload?
While emotional neglect is about absence, **emotional overload** is about *too much*—too much burden, too much responsibility, too many unspoken expectations. It's being the emotional anchor for others while quietly drowning yourself.

This can come from:
- **Carrying others' burdens** constantly without a break.

- **Absorbing emotional pain** from multiple people—family, friends, coworkers.
- **Not knowing how to say "no"**, often because of guilt, fear of rejection, or a deep desire to be needed.
- **Lack of boundaries**, where people feel entitled to your time, energy, and emotional support.

Eventually, when your emotional tank is depleted and demands continue to rise, you start to bleed from within. You smile and function, but inside, you feel crushed. Life becomes colorless, even though everything around you still looks the same.

The Internal Consequences
- **Exhaustion without explanation** – You're tired, but it's not physical. It's soul deep.
- **Detachment or numbness** – You stop feeling because it's the only way to cope.
- **Bitterness or resentment** – You begin to resent those you once loved to serve.
- **Low self-worth** – Constant neglect or overload sends a message that you are only valuable for what you *do*, not for who you *are*.
- **Quiet despair** – A sense of hopelessness that no one really sees or understands you.

How to Begin Healing
- **Acknowledge your pain.** Emotional neglect and overload are real. Don't downplay your experiences or tell yourself to just "be strong." Healing begins with honesty.
- **Set emotional boundaries.** Learn to say "no" without guilt. You are not responsible for carrying everyone's emotions. Protect your peace.

- **Start expressing your needs.** Begin with safe, trusted people. Let them know when you're not okay. Stop hiding your struggles behind smiles.
- **Rest without shame.** Rest is not laziness. Emotional rest is necessary to refill your tank. Create space for silence, solitude, prayer, and self-care.
- **Seek God's comfort.** Isaiah 40:29 says, "He gives strength to the weary and increases the power of the weak." You don't have to carry it all. God sees what others don't. He knows your silent pain and offers a safe place for your weary soul.
- **Reach out for support.** You don't have to walk through emotional neglect or overload alone. Talk to a counselor, mentor, or spiritual leader. Vulnerability can be the first step to freedom.

You are not a machine. You are not an emotional dumpster. You are a person—worthy of love, rest, attention, and care. Don't let the world steal your voice or silence your needs. Your heart matters. Your healing matters. And your soul deserves to breathe again.

Healing from Emotional Bleeding

Emotional bleeding is not always visible, but it's just as real and damaging as a physical wound. You may look fine on the outside—still functioning, still showing up—but inside, you're slowly unraveling. Whether it's the sting of betrayal, the weight of unresolved trauma, or the exhaustion of giving too much and receiving too little, emotional wounds must be acknowledged and intentionally healed. Here's a roadmap to begin that journey:
- **Acknowledge the Wound.** Healing begins with honesty. You can't treat what you pretend doesn't exist. Stop telling

yourself to "just get over it" or that "it wasn't a big deal." It *was* a big deal. God never heals what we're too proud or too afraid to expose. Like David in the Psalms, pour out your heart to God. Admit the hurt. Name the betrayal. Recognize the fatigue. There's no healing in denial—only delay. Jesus never condemned the wounded for bleeding; instead, He extended compassion, and He will do the same for you.

- **Seek Safe Spaces.** Not everyone deserves access to your vulnerability. Healing requires the safety of compassionate community. Surround yourself with people who don't just tolerate your pain but can sit with you in it. These are people who won't rush your process, shame your emotions, or dismiss your experience. Sometimes, it's a friend, mentor, counselor, or even a support group—but find that place where you can breathe, cry, and speak freely. Healing multiplies in healthy company.

- **Rest and Replenish.** Don't underestimate the toll emotional bleeding takes on your body, mind, and spirit. You may need to *pause* from responsibilities or step back from certain roles. Even Jesus, knowing the weight of His mission, often withdrew to solitary places to pray and recharge. Rest isn't laziness, it's obedience. It's giving God space to minister to you. Healing thrives in stillness. Let your soul catch up with your body. Let quietness, worship, and prayer restore what emotional trauma has drained.

- **Speak Up.** Silence can feel safer, but it's a trap. When pain festers in the dark, it turns into bitterness, anxiety, or depression. You were never meant to suffer in silence.

Whether through journaling, counseling, or confiding in a trusted voice, release the weight of your words. Pain named is pain tamed. You don't have to be eloquent—just honest. When you speak, you begin to take your power back. Don't let pride or fear rob you of the freedom that comes through expression.

- **Forgive, But Learn.** Forgiveness is crucial, not just for the offender, but for *you*. Bitterness is emotional poison that slowly kills your peace, joy, and hope. Forgiveness isn't forgetting or excusing—it's choosing to release the offense so your heart can be free. However, healing also involves wisdom. Not every relationship needs to be restored to its former place. Learning means guarding your heart, recognizing red flags, and not re-opening doors that God closed. Forgiveness clears your soul; discernment protects it going forward.

- **Refill Spiritually.** Emotional wounds create spiritual emptiness. You may feel distant from God, numb in worship, or unable to pray. That's okay. But don't stay there. Go back to the well. Even if all you can do is whisper His name—start there. The Word of God is medicine for the soul. Worship is balm for weary hearts. Prayer is oxygen for suffocating emotions. In God's presence, you are reminded of who you are, who He is, and how deeply you are loved—even in your brokenness. His healing often starts where human words end.

- **Establish Boundaries.** Healing doesn't just require looking back, it also requires guarding your future. Begin to set clear emotional boundaries. Learn to say *no* without explanation or guilt. Protect your peace, time, and energy. Just because you're healed doesn't mean you're invincible. Recovery still needs reinforcement. You have the right to limit access, walk away from toxic environments, and distance yourself from people who continue to reopen old wounds. Healing includes learning to preserve what God has restored.

Tend to Your Soul. You cannot *lead*, *love*, or *live* fully while emotionally bleeding. Wounded hearts cannot pour into others without bleeding out. If you've been hurt by betrayal, crushed under the weight of leadership, or hollowed out by emotional neglect, know this: healing is possible. Your pain is not invisible to God. He promises in Psalm 147:3, *"He heals the brokenhearted and binds up their wounds."*

Don't ignore the warning signs. Don't normalize inner exhaustion. Don't let your soul bleed out while the world sees you smile. Healing doesn't happen overnight, but it does happen—when we turn to the One who sees our pain, welcomes our tears, and binds our wounds with divine compassion.

CHAPTER 5
Spiritual Bleeding

Spiritual bleeding is the silent, internal hemorrhaging of a soul that once burned with fire for God but now struggles under the weight of unseen wounds. It's especially dangerous because it's often hidden beneath the surface of public service, performance, and leadership roles in ministry.

1. Feeling Far from God While Leading His People
There is a painful and often hidden paradox in being used by God to bless others while personally feeling spiritually dry, disconnected, or distant from Him. This is a burden many leaders quietly carry — the weight of spiritual responsibility while privately feeling empty. It is possible, and even common, to be on fire in public ministry while flickering in personal devotion. You can preach sermons that stir souls, pray prayers that shake atmospheres, and speak words of life into broken hearts — all while secretly wrestling with silence from heaven.

This internal dissonance can be unsettling. You find yourself pouring out from a place you're no longer drawing from. Your hands are busy doing the work of God, but your heart aches for the presence of the God of the work. This form of spiritual bleeding is subtle, yet dangerous, because it operates under the mask of effectiveness. Ministry may still be fruitful, but the root is quietly withering.

Unchecked, this creates a spiritual vacuum filled with guilt, shame, and an increasing sense of hypocrisy. You begin to wonder: *How can I preach about intimacy with God when I feel like a stranger in prayer? How can I guide others into truth when I myself feel lost in shadows?* These haunting questions begin to erode your sense of identity, value, and calling.

The result? Bitterness can grow where joy once bloomed. Burnout replaces passion. Isolation becomes a preferred refuge over authentic vulnerability. The enemy of your soul whispers lies: *You're a fraud. God is done with you. You're only useful, not loved.* And in the absence of regular, refreshing communion with God, those lies start sounding like truth.

This is not a new struggle. Scripture is filled with examples: Moses led a stiff-necked people while crying out to see God's glory. Elijah called down fire but later begged for death in a cave. David, the man after God's own heart, penned psalms of anguish and distance. Even Jesus, in His humanity, experienced the pain of feeling forsaken on the cross.

The solution is not to quit ministry, but to return to intimacy. To prioritize your sonship over your service. Ministry is not meant to replace your relationship with God—it must flow from it. The first calling of every leader is not to the pulpit or platform, but to the presence of God. Without it, we risk becoming functional orphans: doing God's work disconnected from God's voice.

Here are a few reminders for leaders in such seasons:
- **Be honest with God** – He is not intimidated by your silence, questions, or fatigue. Pour out your heart. He already knows.

- **Rebuild your altar** – Go back to simple communion. Not sermons. Not studies. Just sit with Him.
- **Stop performing** – God didn't call you to perform; He called you to be His. Let go of striving.
- **Seek accountability** – Find trusted spiritual friends or mentors who can walk with you in truth and grace.
- **Rest without guilt** – You are not God. You are not the source. Your worth is not in your output.

When leaders take the risk to confess their emptiness, they create space for God to fill them afresh. It's not shameful to need Him—it's dangerous to try leading without Him. Let your first ministry be your heart. From that place, everything else finds alignment.

2. Ministry Without Intimacy

Ministry without intimacy is like drawing water from a dry well—eventually, there's nothing left to give. It is the subtle yet dangerous shift from presence to performance, where the work of ministry becomes a substitute for the God of the ministry. This is when a leader becomes more preoccupied with the **tasks of God** than with **time with God**, mistaking busyness for fruitfulness and public success for spiritual health.

A schedule packed with appointments, meetings, and programs may impress people, but it does not impress God. Heaven is not moved by motion; it is moved by **devotion**. When leaders neglect the secret place—that holy ground where hearts are aligned, burdens are exchanged, and divine instructions are received—they become vulnerable to burnout, pride, and disillusionment.

Ministry becomes mechanical. It's easy to fall into autopilot mode, operating on yesterday's anointing and relying on natural charisma or learned skills. But the power of ministry is never in the vessel itself — it is in the One who fills the vessel. And when the vessel is not continually filled, it eventually runs dry.

This is why Jesus is our ultimate model. Though He had the most urgent mission in history — to seek and save the lost—He never allowed ministry demands to rob Him of intimacy with the Father. The Gospels reveal that Jesus **withdrew often to pray** (Mark 1:35; Luke 5:16). He wasn't running on the momentum of miracles; He was constantly recharged by communion. His public power was directly tied to His private prayer.

Without this kind of intimacy, ministry becomes unsustainable. The soul becomes parched, the mind overloaded, and the heart distant from the One we claim to represent. Soon, we find ourselves feeding people from emptiness, offering words without weight and actions without anointing.

A spiritually dry leader cannot nourish a spiritually hungry people. The result is a generation fed with secondhand fire—warmed by passion but not purified by presence. Worse still, ministry can descend into manipulation, using God's name to push personal agendas or build platforms that no longer reflect His heart.

This is the tragedy of ministry without intimacy: it may **start in the Spirit**, but if not anchored in daily relationship, it will **end in the flesh** (Galatians 3:3). Titles replace testimony. Strategy replaces surrender. And influence replaces obedience.

Let this be a solemn call: before we speak for God, we must sit with Him. Before we build for God, we must behold Him. Our first ministry is to the Lord Himself (Ezekiel 44:15-16), not the stage, not the people, not the platform.

True ministry flows from **overflow**, not obligation. It is birthed in the **secret place**, not in the spotlight. The oil that touches others must first be poured out in our personal time with God. Without this, we risk leading people to altars we no longer kneel at ourselves.

So, return. Come back to the feet of Jesus. Let your identity be found not in what you do for Him, but in who you are with Him. Because it is only from the **deep well of intimacy** that **true ministry flows**.

3. When Prayers Feel Unanswered for the Leader

One of the most painful and confusing seasons in the life of any spiritual leader is when they intercede for others and witness breakthroughs, yet their own heartfelt prayers appear to go unanswered. They lay hands on the sick and see healing. They speak words of prophecy and clarity into the lives of others. Marriages are restored, doors are opened, and testimonies abound—all around them. But when they return to their own prayer closet, it can feel eerily quiet. Heaven, which seems so responsive on behalf of others, suddenly appears closed and unyielding to their own desperate cries.

This is not just discouraging; it is deeply wounding. It creates a type of internal spiritual bleeding—a quiet agony that is hard to articulate. While others are publicly rejoicing over answered prayers and divine interventions, the leader may be silently grappling with personal pain, disappointment, unanswered questions, or long-standing struggles that seem resistant to prayer and fasting. And yet, the calling remains: to preach with passion, to lead with conviction, to counsel with wisdom, and to serve with a smile.

The burden of leadership is often accompanied by the paradox of public strength and private weakness. The leader is expected to inspire faith while wrestling with doubt, to offer hope while managing their own heartbreak, and to keep pouring out even when they feel empty inside. The weight of responsibility doesn't pause for personal battles. Ministry continues. Needs don't wait. People keep coming.

In such seasons, feelings can become deceptive. Silence can feel like abandonment. Delay can feel like denial. And isolation can feel like punishment. But this is where the leader must make a crucial decision—to anchor in **faith, not feelings**. Feelings fluctuate. Faith stands firm. Faith declares, "God is still good," even when nothing looks good. Faith says, "God is still working," even when nothing seems to be moving.

The silence of God is not the absence of God. Sometimes His silence is His strategy. He is not ignoring the leader; He is refining them. He is doing a deeper work—not through the external answers, but through internal surrender. The wilderness is not a punishment; it is a proving ground. It's the place where the leader's intimacy with God is forged, not through applause, but through abiding. Not through visibility, but through vulnerability. Not through blessings, but through brokenness.

In the Bible, even the greatest leaders experienced this. Elijah called down fire from heaven but later sat under a broom tree in deep despair, feeling abandoned. David was anointed as king but spent years in caves, crying out to God in anguish. Paul performed miracles yet pleaded three times for his own "thorn" to be removed—and it wasn't. Even Jesus, in the Garden of Gethsemane, prayed with such agony that His sweat became like drops of blood, asking for the cup to pass—yet it did not. These moments were not signs of divine neglect, but of divine intimacy and purpose.

So, to the leader who feels unseen and unheard, know this: **God sees. God hears. God cares.** The delay is not a denial—it's a deepening. He is building endurance. He is solidifying trust. He is shaping character. And most importantly, He is drawing you closer—not because of what He gives, but because of who He is.

In time, you will look back and realize that those "unanswered" prayers were actually answered most profoundly—by making you more like Christ. The silence formed you. The waiting humbled you. The pain purified you. And through it all, God was not preparing a blessing for you—**He was preparing you for the blessing.**

Stay faithful, leader. The God who answers for others will answer for you — in His time, in His way, and for His glory.

Healing the Bleeding

There comes a point in ministry where you realize that even those who pour into others can be running on empty. Spiritual bleeding is real—it may not leave visible scars, but it drains the soul quietly, silently, until strength fades, passion wanes, and burnout sets in like a thief in the night. If left unaddressed, it becomes a silent killer, robbing you of joy, clarity, and intimacy with God. But there is hope. The Healer of the brokenhearted—the One you proclaim to others—is still near. He longs to restore you. He sees your wounds even when no one else does. You don't have to bleed out in silence. It's time to return to the place where it all began—the secret place.

1. Return to the Secret Place
Before there were pulpits and platforms, there was presence. Before you were called to preach, you were called to sit at His feet. The secret place isn't a workspace for sermon crafting—it's a sanctuary for soul healing. Go back there. Not to find a message, but to find *Him*. Let your heart be still again. Worship with no agenda. Wait in silence. If you must, weep. Cry out. Allow your tears to speak what words cannot. In that holy stillness, He will refill what life and ministry have drained. That sacred space is not optional — it is vital for your survival.

2. Be Vulnerable and Transparent
Isolation is one of the enemy's favorite tactics against those in spiritual leadership. It whispers, *"You can't show weakness. They won't understand."* But healing comes through light. Find those you trust—spiritual mentors, seasoned counselors, or faithful peers. Open your heart. Share your wounds, your weariness, your questions. You don't need to bleed behind closed doors when God has placed safe, Spirit-led people in your life to walk with you. Confession doesn't make you weak — it makes you whole. Vulnerability is the doorway to divine healing.

3. Rest and Retreat Intentionally

Jesus Himself, though filled with power and mission, told His disciples, *"Come away by yourselves to a desolate place and rest a while"* (Mark 6:31). If the Son of God saw rest as essential, why do we treat it as optional? Ministry must not become a treadmill that runs us ragged. Your soul needs space to breathe again free from meetings, demands, expectations, and spiritual performance. Schedule rest the way you schedule ministry—with intentionality and reverence. A retreat isn't a luxury; it's an act of obedience for the weary. Don't just rest your body — rest your soul.

4. Receive Ministry, Don't Just Give It

Sometimes the greatest act of humility is not giving but receiving. You were never meant to be only a dispenser of spiritual nourishment. Sit down. Listen to a sermon not to critique, but to be fed. Stand at the altar, not as a minister, but as a child in need. Allow others to anoint, counsel, and pray over you. You are not less spiritual because you need ministry; you are more human. Jesus washed the feet of His disciples, and He still washes ours. Let someone pour oil over your wounds. Let someone else carry the weight for a moment.

5. Remember Your Identity

You are not your calling. You are not your gifts, your sermons, your church size, or your spiritual productivity. Before you ever stepped onto a stage, you were God's child—loved, chosen, and called by name. Ministry is what you *do*, but it is not who you *are*. Your greatest value is not in your output, but in your intimacy with the Father. If you lost every platform, would you still know your worth? Heaven's applause is louder than any congregation's.

Return to the arms of the Father, where your identity is not in performance, but in relationship.

The Healer is Still Near

Spiritual bleeding doesn't have to end in collapse. The same Jesus who healed the woman with the issue of blood—silently suffering for twelve years— still walks among His servants. He notices what others miss. He feels what others don't. And He is still able to say, *"Daughter, son, your faith has made you well. Go in peace."* Don't hide your wounds behind your work. Come back to the One who called you. Let Him mend your heart, renew your strength, and revive your purpose. Because no servant of God should die trying to serve Him. Healing begins in His presence.

CHAPTER 6
Mental Bleeding

Mental bleeding is a silent struggle—an emotional and psychological wound that doesn't bleed externally but drains internally. It describes the invisible battles people fight within the corridors of their minds, often while appearing composed on the outside. These inner wounds, if left unacknowledged, can cripple confidence, cloud judgment, and rob a person of peace and clarity. Mental bleeding doesn't always scream; sometimes, it whispers in the form of subtle dysfunction, unchecked fear, and silent exhaustion.

Anxiety, Depression, and Internal Battles
Anxiety is far more than simple worry or nervousness. It's a relentless mental storm—an invisible hurricane that spins even minor issues into catastrophes. It plays scenarios on loop in the mind, convincing the sufferer that the worst is always about to happen. It tightens the chest, quickens the heartbeat, and fogs the ability to think clearly. To those living with it, peace often feels like a distant memory, and rest—even when achieved—never seems truly restful. The constant need to appear composed can be exhausting, and often, anxiety hides behind perfectionism, busyness, and overachievement.

Depression, in contrast, feels like the color has been drained from life. It's the silent weight that makes getting out of bed feel like climbing a mountain. Joy, motivation, and purpose can feel like distant echoes. Once simple tasks become insurmountable. It can feel like moving through molasses, with the world passing by while one remains stuck in place. And yet, many people with depression still smile, still function, and still go unnoticed—because depression can wear the mask of normalcy remarkably well. It is an internal grief that doesn't always cry out loud but hurts deeply and persistently.

Internal battles are the unseen wars we fight within ourselves—often daily, often in silence. These battles are not merely emotional fluctuations; they are deeply rooted struggles tied to identity, self-worth, trauma, and personal expectations. They include the fight between who we are and who we think we should be; between the voice of self-criticism and the longing for grace; between the shame of past mistakes and the hunger for forgiveness and healing. These battles don't always have external symptoms, but they leave scars—mental, emotional, and spiritual.

They can show up as the persistent feeling of not being enough, the fear of being truly known, or the inner voice that whispers failure even in the face of success. Internal battles can sabotage relationships, hinder personal growth, and create a disconnect between one's external life and inner reality.

Together, **anxiety, depression, and internal battles** form a trio that many people carry alone—often unnoticed, misunderstood, or minimized. That's why empathy matters. That's why asking, "How are you?" should go beyond formality. That's why checking in, listening without judgment, and encouraging open conversations about mental health are not just kind gestures; they are acts of courage and compassion.

Healing is possible, but it begins with acknowledgment. It begins when we recognize that not all wounds bleed and that not all battles are fought on visible battlefields. The more we speak, the less shame has power. The more we understand, the more we can help. And the more we extend grace—to others and to ourselves—the closer we come to wholeness.

Impostor Syndrome in Leadership

Leadership is often perceived as a domain of strength, certainty, and competence. From the outside, leaders are expected to be decisive, confident, and in control. Yet, beneath the surface, many leaders are silently battling a deeply rooted internal struggle—**impostor syndrome**.

Impostor syndrome is the persistent inner dialogue that insists, *"You're a fraud,"* despite clear evidence of competence and success. It's the subtle, undermining whisper that surfaces in boardrooms, during public speeches, or in moments of recognition: *"You don't belong here."* While colleagues may see a poised and accomplished leader, the internal experience can feel like walking a tightrope, fearful of making a misstep that will finally reveal one's perceived inadequacy.

This psychological pattern is a silent predator that ambushes leaders, especially high-achieving ones. It creeps in during decision-making, when the weight of responsibility triggers self-doubt. It shows up after a big win, causing the leader to minimize their success as luck or timing rather than skill or hard work. It thrives in environments where expectations are high and vulnerability are scarce.

Leaders with impostor syndrome often:

- **Downplay their accomplishments**, attributing them to external factors rather than personal merit.
- **Overwork and over-prepare**, trying to compensate for what they believe they lack.
- **Fear failure excessively**, seeing it not as a learning opportunity, but as confirmation of their unworthiness.
- **Avoid new opportunities**, not because of a lack of ability, but because of the fear of being exposed as "not good enough."

Over time, this mental battle can erode confidence, distort self-perception, and cap leadership potential. It fosters a dangerous cycle of perfectionism, fear of failure, and self-sabotage. Even when they achieve remarkable results, leaders may feel like they're only "acting" the part, constantly anxious about when the curtain will fall.

But impostor syndrome doesn't have to be a life sentence in leadership.

The first step toward freedom is **acknowledgment**. Recognizing that these feelings are common—even among top performers—is powerful. In fact, research shows that many renowned leaders, CEOs, and public figures have wrestled with the same internal insecurities.

Next comes **reframing the narrative**. Instead of interpreting success as a fluke, leaders can learn to internalize positive feedback and reflect on their journey with honesty and gratitude. Embracing vulnerability, seeking mentorship, and surrounding oneself with a support system that speaks truth to the mind's lies can also be healing.

Furthermore, organizations can help by **creating cultures that normalize struggle**, reward authenticity, and support leadership development that includes emotional intelligence and self-awareness.

True leadership isn't the absence of doubt—it's the courage to lead despite it. The most effective leaders are not those who never question themselves, but those who learn to lead while silencing the impostor within.

Decision Fatigue and Overthinking
In today's fast-paced world, we are constantly bombarded with choices—from what to eat for breakfast to complex life-altering decisions about careers, relationships, and personal values. While freedom of choice is often celebrated as a sign of progress and autonomy, it can also become a mental burden. **Decision fatigue** is the psychological weariness that sets in after making countless choices, especially when those decisions carry emotional or high-stakes weight. Over time, this mental exhaustion impairs judgment, decreases self-control, and leads to a tendency to either avoid making decisions altogether or make poor ones.

At its core, decision fatigue isn't about laziness or incompetence. It's the brain's natural response to overload. Just like a muscle, the mind gets tired when it's overused. Each choice, no matter how small, demands cognitive effort. The more decisions we make, the harder it becomes to weigh options objectively. This is why many people find themselves zoning out at the end of the day, deferring important decisions, or opting for the easiest—not necessarily the best—option.

Running parallel to decision fatigue is **overthinking**, a chronic mental loop that masquerades as being thoughtful or meticulous. But rather than leading to clarity, overthinking traps the mind in endless cycles of doubt, "what ifs," and imagined consequences. It feeds on fear—fear of failure, fear of making the wrong choice, fear of judgment. The result is paralysis. Actions are delayed or completely avoided under the illusion of seeking more information or waiting for the "perfect" moment. Over time, this not only wastes valuable time and energy but also breeds regret and missed opportunities.

Overthinking and decision fatigue together create a toxic mental environment. They slowly erode confidence and clarity. You begin to second-guess yourself, distrust your instincts, and fear outcomes before they even happen. What was once a simple task becomes a mental battlefield. The energy that could be used for creativity, growth, and progress is consumed by internal friction, a kind of **emotional and cognitive internal bleeding**. This invisible drain can go unnoticed for a long time, manifesting as procrastination, anxiety, low productivity, emotional detachment, or burnout.

Breaking Free
To combat decision fatigue and overthinking, intentional boundaries and routines are key. Here are a few ways to reclaim your mental strength:
1. **Simplify Low-Stakes Choices:** Reduce the number of daily trivial decisions. This could mean planning meals, setting a morning routine, or wearing a simplified wardrobe. The less mental energy spent on minor choices, the more bandwidth you preserve for important ones.

2. **Set Time Limits on Decisions:** Don't give yourself unlimited time to think. Timed decision-making forces action and prevents mental spirals.
3. **Learn to Trust Yourself:** Not every decision requires excessive analysis. Learn to trust your values, experience, and instincts. You won't always get it right, but progress is better than perfection.
4. **Practice Mindfulness:** Becoming aware of your thought patterns can help break the overthinking loop. Meditation, journaling, or simply pausing to breathe can anchor you in the present.
5. **Limit Information Intake:** Constant information consumption can lead to analysis paralysis. Curate what you read or watch and be selective about your sources.
6. **Prioritize Rest and Recovery:** Mental fatigue thrives in overworked, sleep-deprived minds. Make rest a non-negotiable part of your routine.

Decision fatigue and overthinking are not signs of weakness—they are reflections of the overwhelming world we navigate. But they don't have to dominate our lives. By creating structure, embracing imperfection, and being mindful of how we manage our thoughts and choices, we can reclaim clarity, energy, and peace of mind. The goal isn't to make perfect decisions, but to stay mentally healthy and present enough to make consistent, good ones.

Healing the Bleeding Mind
Mental bleeding is an invisible wound—one that doesn't always manifest in ways the world can see, but one that deeply affects how we think, feel, lead, and live. It is the slow leak of inner

peace, hope, and clarity. It is the silent suffering that many carry behind forced smiles, constant busyness, or emotional numbness. Healing from such internal wounds requires intentional, ongoing care. It is not passive. It is not instant. But it is absolutely possible.

Recognizing the Signs

Healing begins with awareness. Mental bleeding often starts with subtle symptoms: chronic exhaustion, emotional irritability, lack of motivation, or a deep sense of emptiness. It can manifest as anxiety that won't settle, a heaviness that sleep doesn't lift, or a lack of interest in what once brought joy. Recognizing these signs isn't weakness—it's wisdom. It's the first brave step toward recovery.

Refusing to Suffer in Silence

One of the greatest lies mental affliction tells us is that we must endure it alone. But silence is not strength—silence is suffocation. Healing begins when we permit ourselves to speak up, to admit we're not okay, and to ask for help. Vulnerability is not a flaw; it is the doorway to freedom. When we share our pain in safe, trusted spaces, we release the power it has over us.

Embracing Rest and Reflection

Rest is not a luxury; it's a necessity. Our minds, like our bodies, need rhythms of rest to recover. For leaders, this means learning to slow down, to delegate, and to recognize that constant output without input leads to burnout. For individuals, it means carving out time for stillness, reflection, and soul-care. Journaling, prayer, nature walks, therapy, and spiritual retreats can all serve as vehicles of restoration.

Distinguishing Thoughts from Truth
Mental bleeding often distorts reality. It convinces us of lies — that we are failures, unlovable, forgotten, or broken beyond repair. But thoughts are not always truths. Part of healing is learning to separate passing mental storms from permanent identity. We must challenge harmful narratives with affirming truths: *I am loved. I am healing. I am not alone. I am enough.*

Creating Safe Spaces
Healing is hindered in toxic environments. Whether it's a demanding workplace, a critical relationship, or a spiritually empty space, we must seek—or create—environments that nurture rather than drain. Safe spaces aren't just physical—they are emotional and spiritual too. Surround yourself with those who listen without judgment, encourage growth, and affirm your humanity.

The Power of Support and Grace
No one heals alone. Professional counselors, spiritual mentors, honest friends, and a community that embraces brokenness can be lifelines in the healing journey. And we must also extend grace to ourselves—to recover at our own pace, to have bad days without guilt, and to celebrate small victories. Healing is not linear, but it is sacred.

Mental bleeding is real, but it is not final. With intentionality, awareness, and the courage to seek help, the bleeding can stop. The mind can be renewed. Joy can return. And peace—lasting, deep, soul-level peace—can be restored.

CHAPTER 7
Physical Bleeding

"Physical bleeding" doesn't always refer to the literal loss of blood. It can also describe the slow, unnoticed drain of strength, health, and vitality caused by living in constant overdrive. Many people are silently bleeding, physically drained, depleted, and deteriorating—because they ignore the signals of their bodies in the name of purpose, ambition, or even ministry.

Exhaustion and Sickness from Overwork
In today's hyper-productive, achievement-oriented world, exhaustion is often mistaken for excellence. Society praises those who burn the midnight oil, wear multiple hats, and constantly grind without pause. Long hours, missed meals, and sleep deprivation are worn as medals of honor—as if the more drained you are, the more worthy and successful you must be. Unfortunately, this glorification of busyness and overwork comes at a heavy price.

While hard work is noble and diligence is biblical, chronic overwork crosses a line. When the body is pushed beyond its natural capacity for prolonged periods, it begins to revolt. What starts as tiredness soon morphs into mental fog, emotional instability, weakened immunity, frequent illness, and eventually, total burnout. Many individuals who find themselves constantly sick, emotionally drained, or spiritually dry may not be under demonic attack; they're simply breaking down under the weight of an unsustainable lifestyle.

God created our physical bodies with built-in limits and rhythms for a reason. We were never meant to operate like machines. Even the most advanced devices need regular maintenance, rest, and cooling time to function properly. How much more should human beings, who are complex, emotional, spiritual, and physical creatures, honor the necessity of rest and renewal?

The principle of rest is not just practical—it's sacred. God Himself modeled it. After six days of creation, the Almighty rested on the seventh, not because He was tired, but to set a precedent. He wove rest into the very fabric of creation. The Sabbath was instituted not as a burden but as a gift—a weekly reminder that our worth is not measured by how much we do, but by who we are in Him.

When we continuously override our limits, we dishonor the design of our Creator. Sleep deprivation, skipped meals, neglected exercise, and chronic stress not only damage our health but also dull our spiritual sensitivity. Exhaustion makes it harder to hear God, to love others well, and to live joyfully. It shrinks our capacity to be present and steals the emotional margin we need for meaningful relationships.

Working hard is not wrong; it's honorable and often necessary. But it must be balanced with wisdom, stewardship, and rest. Taking care of your body is not laziness; it's obedience. Rest is not a sign of weakness; it's a spiritual discipline. Protecting your health is not selfish; it's preparation to serve longer, love better, and live fully.

So, if you're always tired, constantly sick, or emotionally numb, pause and assess: Is this spiritual warfare, or is your body simply sounding the alarm? Take a step back. Rebuild your rhythms. Embrace rest. Remember: your body is not a machine, and even machines break down without care.

Ignoring the Body in the Name of Purpose
In the pursuit of divine calling and purpose, many passionate individuals fall into the dangerous trap of neglecting their physical well-being. They equate diligence with the denial of rest, and sacrifice with the absence of self-care. Somewhere along the way, they have embraced the lie that exhaustion equals spirituality, and that burning the candle at both ends is a badge of holy devotion. But nothing could be further from the truth.

God never called us to destroy the vessel to fulfill the vision. The body is not the enemy of purpose—it is the carrier of it. When we ignore our physical needs under the guise of purpose, we are not being spiritual; we are being irresponsible. True spiritual maturity involves understanding that our health is part of our calling. When God formed us, He made us spirit, soul, and body—not spirit alone. Each part matters to Him, and each must be cared for intentionally.

Many confuse *self-denial* with *self-destruction*. Yes, Scripture calls us to carry our cross, to die to fleshly desires, and to put God's will above our own. But it does not call us to abuse ourselves in the name of obedience. Jesus, our perfect example, withdrew to rest. He slept in storms, withdrew from crowds, and prioritized solitude—teaching us that rest is not laziness; it is wisdom. If the

Savior of the world knew when to pause, who are we to ignore that rhythm?

There is a subtle pride in refusing to acknowledge our human limits. When we consistently override the signals of our bodies—chronic fatigue, headaches, emotional burnout, weakened immunity—we are not just being unwise; we are being disobedient. God designed our bodies with built-in warning systems. Ignoring those signs isn't faith—it's foolishness. Pushing beyond boundaries for prolonged periods doesn't glorify God; it only shortens the lifespan of your assignment.

Stewarding your health is part of honoring your purpose. You cannot pour out effectively from an empty cup. A sick, broken, or exhausted vessel cannot consistently do the work of the kingdom. And while God can restore what's broken, He also calls us to steward what He has already given. We are temples of the Holy Spirit—not rundown tents to be discarded but sanctuaries to be preserved and protected.

Let's stop glamorizing burnout. Being busy is not the same as being fruitful. Overworking isn't always a sign of commitment—it may be a symptom of insecurity, people-pleasing, or misplaced identity. We must learn to rest as an act of trust, knowing that God sustains the vision even when we sleep.

In all our getting—get purpose, yes. But also get wisdom. Take care of your body. Sleep. Eat well. Move regularly. Laugh. Pause. Breathe. These are not carnal indulgences; they are acts of worship when done in reverence to God.

Remember: **Your body is not a burden to purpose; it is the bridge to fulfilling it.** Treat it as such.

God's Design for Rest
Rest is not laziness; it is obedience. In Genesis, God created the world in six days and rested on the seventh—not because He was tired, but to set a pattern. Rest was part of creation's rhythm. It was so important that God commanded His people to observe the Sabbath—not as a burden, but as a gift.

Jesus also modeled rest. He took time away from the crowds to pray, sleep, and eat. He told His disciples, "Come away by yourselves to a desolate place and rest a while" (Mark 6:31). If the Son of God needed rest in the flesh, how much more do we?

Rest is not the absence of productivity; it is the refueling that makes sustainable productivity possible. Neglecting rest in the name of ministry, work, or ambition is not spiritual—it is reckless. God is not glorified when we collapse from exhaustion.

Your body is not an enemy of purpose—it is a vessel of it. Taking care of your health, honoring your body's need for rest, and avoiding the trap of overwork is not weakness but wisdom. Don't bleed yourself dry in the name of drive. Protect the temple God gave you so you can run your race with endurance and finish well.

PART THREE: THE PRESSURE TO PRETEND

CHAPTER 8
The Mask of Strength

Unpacking the Pressure of Performance in Leadership
In today's leadership landscape, there is an unspoken expectation to always appear strong, composed, and in control. This is especially true in performance-driven environments where results matter more than emotional well-being. The pressure to perform can become a breeding ground for what we can call *"The Mask of Strength"*—a façade leaders wear to project confidence and resilience, even when they are internally struggling.

1. Performance Culture in Leadership
In today's fast-paced, results-driven world, leadership is often measured by visible, quantifiable outcomes—productivity, profitability, strategic wins, innovation, and influence. These benchmarks are undeniably important. They provide a framework for growth, accountability, and vision fulfillment. However, the heavy emphasis on these metrics has gradually fostered a **performance culture**—one that elevates results over **relational authenticity**, external validation over internal well-being, and efficiency over empathy.

In such a culture, leaders are celebrated for what they achieve but rarely given the space to be **fully human**. Vulnerability, emotional fatigue, and seasons of uncertainty are often perceived as liabilities rather than natural aspects of the human experience. This expectation subtly but powerfully pushes leaders into a role that requires not just competence, but **perpetual emotional perfection**. Instead of being seen as whole people, they are expected to be symbols of strength, clarity, and confidence at all times.

This creates a dangerous environment where leaders feel compelled to wear masks—masks of certainty, endless energy, and unshakeable confidence. Behind these facades, many wrestle silently with stress, anxiety, imposter syndrome, or even moral conflict, all while continuing to perform outwardly. The pressure to "keep producing" leads to **emotional suppression**, isolation, and, eventually, **burnout**.

Burnout doesn't always announce itself with a dramatic collapse. Often, it creeps in quietly—through chronic fatigue, decreased empathy, declining motivation, or the subtle erosion of passion. But because the performance culture rarely makes room for these warning signs, leaders often ignore or hide them. They fear that if they admit struggle, they risk being perceived as incompetent or inadequate. Thus, their identity becomes fused with their **output**, not their essence. They become human *doings* rather than human *beings*.

This mindset is not only damaging to the individual leader but also to their teams and organizations. When leaders are not allowed—or do not allow themselves—to be authentic, it sets a tone that vulnerability is weakness. This stifles psychological safety across the organization. Teams mirror what they see: overwork, emotional disconnection, and the silent belief that success is the only acceptable state of being.

To counteract this, a **new model of leadership** must emerge—one that embraces both **performance and authenticity**. True leadership is not about having all the answers or always being strong; it's about cultivating trust, modeling healthy boundaries, and knowing when to ask for help. It's about showing that **strength includes softness**, and that **courage includes the willingness to be seen** in seasons of struggle.

Cultivating this kind of leadership culture means intentionally dismantling the glorification of hustle and hyper-productivity. It means celebrating not just results, but resilience. Not just innovation, but integrity. It requires organizations to create environments where rest is respected, emotional intelligence is prioritized, and leaders are supported as **whole people**.

Ultimately, leaders who lead from a place of authenticity—who refuse to let performance define their worth—don't just thrive personally. They create healthier, more sustainable, and more humane cultures for everyone they lead.

2. Faking Strength to Inspire Others

In many leadership circles, there's an unspoken rule: *Never let them see you sweat.* Leaders, whether in business, ministry, education, or family life, often feel an immense pressure to appear invincible. They adopt the mindset: "If they see me break, they might lose hope." While this belief may stem from a place of responsibility and genuine care for others, it can become a dangerous and unsustainable way of leading.

Wearing the mask of constant strength might seem noble on the surface—it communicates confidence, resolve, and control. But over time, this façade becomes a prison. Leaders who continually fake strength often begin to lose touch with their authentic selves. They suppress their emotions, avoid vulnerable conversations, and internalize stress rather than process it. In the short term, they may be applauded for their resilience, but in the long run, this pattern leads to isolation, emotional exhaustion, burnout, and even breakdown.

The truth is, people do look to leaders for direction and stability—but they do not need a perfect image. What they truly need is *relatable* and *trustworthy* leadership. They need to see strength in a form that is real, not rehearsed. There is a critical distinction between strength and stoicism. **Stoicism hides pain; strength faces it.** Real strength is not the absence of struggle; it's the presence of courage in the midst of it.

Leaders who model authentic vulnerability send a powerful message: *You don't have to be flawless to lead, and you don't have to have it all together to make a difference.* When leaders have the humility to say, "I don't know," "I'm struggling," or "I need help," they don't lose credibility—they gain it. They show others what it means to be emotionally healthy and human.

Ironically, faking strength often leads to disconnection, while *sharing struggles in wise and appropriate ways* builds deeper connection. Vulnerability fosters trust. It creates a culture where others feel safe to be honest about their own challenges, which ultimately builds a more supportive and high-functioning team.

This doesn't mean leaders should emotionally dump on those they lead or abandon their role of guidance during crises. Rather, it means leading with balance—projecting hope while also being honest about the journey. Strength isn't about having no cracks;

it's about being courageous enough to be real even when the pressure says otherwise.

In the end, the most inspiring leaders are not the ones who pretend to have it all together, but the ones who lead from a place of wholeness, integrity, and transparency. **They don't fake strength—they redefine it.**

3. When Vulnerability Feels Like Betrayal of Duty

One of the most intense internal battles for any leader, whether in the workplace, ministry, home, or public sphere, is the persistent belief that vulnerability is weakness and that to show any sign of struggle is to betray the very essence of their leadership. Admitting fear, confusion, fatigue, or emotional pain can feel like a failure to uphold the mantle of strength others expect them to carry. Especially in high-stakes environments where teams, families, or entire organizations are looking to them for direction and stability, the unspoken pressure is heavy: *"They need me to be strong. I cannot afford to falter. I cannot let them down."*

But this pressure, while understandable, is often rooted in a fundamental misunderstanding of leadership itself. True leadership is not about flawless performance or emotional invincibility. It's about courage, integrity, and relational wisdom. It's about being present, authentic, and grounded—not just in success, but also in struggle. Leadership done well is not about hiding scars; it's about knowing when and how to reveal them in ways that inspire healing and connection rather than fear or chaos.

Vulnerability, when expressed with discernment, is not a betrayal of leadership; it is one of its most powerful tools. A leader who acknowledges their humanity without abdicating their responsibility becomes a safe space for others. When a leader says, *"This is hard for me too,"* or *"I don't have all the answers, but I'm committed to finding a way forward,"* they model a kind of strength that is deeper than bravado—it is rooted in truth. They cultivate an environment where team members, employees, or even family members feel seen and invited into honest dialogue. This kind of leadership builds trust, fosters resilience, and nurtures psychological safety.

Unfortunately, many leaders have never seen this modeled. They were taught, implicitly or explicitly, that leadership means stoicism, silence, and self-denial. They were shown that emotions are liabilities, and that expressing pain or uncertainty makes you less credible, less capable, or less godly. And so, they learn to suffer in silence. They wear a mask of strength that feels noble at first—but slowly suffocates the soul. The longer this mask is worn, the more isolated and disconnected the leader becomes—not only from others, but also from their own heart, and sometimes even from God.

Spiritual disconnection is especially dangerous. Leaders who constantly push through their exhaustion without rest or honest prayer begin to confuse performance with purpose. They become so focused on "holding everything together" that they miss the whisper of God inviting them to come undone in His presence. Vulnerability before God is not just permitted—it is necessary. Even Jesus, the greatest leader of all time, wept publicly, expressed anguish in Gethsemane, and cried out on the cross. He did not hide His humanity; He modeled holy dependence.

If Jesus could lead with vulnerability, then surely we can too.

There is wisdom, of course, in how and when to be vulnerable. Not all emotions should be shared with everyone. A leader must discern the difference between vulnerability and oversharing—between inviting connection and creating confusion. But when done well, vulnerability becomes a sacred act of leadership. It says to those around you: *You are not alone in your struggle. We can walk through this together.*

So, to the leader who feels torn between authenticity and duty, remember this: your vulnerability is not a liability; it is part of your legacy. Your team, your family, your community—they don't need a perfect leader. They need a real one

The Way Forward: Authentic Leadership

In a culture that often glorifies image over integrity and performance over presence, leaders are frequently pressured to wear a mask, projecting strength while hiding struggles, radiating confidence while concealing fears. But the way forward for leadership today is not through perfect façades or curated personas; it's through courageous authenticity.

To remove the mask of strength is not to become weak—it is to become whole. Wholeness means integrating all parts of who we are: the strong and the struggling, the clear and the confused, the confident and the questioning. True leadership is not about denying these tensions but embracing them with humility and grace. Leaders must understand that **authenticity is not an obstacle to influence—it is the foundation of it.**

Strength and vulnerability are not opposites; they are allies. Vulnerability does not diminish a leader's power; it refines it. When strength is rooted in self-awareness and tempered by transparency, it fosters trust. Real leaders lead from the **inside out**, not from behind a mask. Their influence flows not just from what they do, but from **who they are**.

To break free from the exhausting performance trap and step into authentic leadership, several intentional steps are needed:

1. Redefine Strength
True strength is not about having all the answers or appearing unshakable. It's about being **grounded, centered, and honest**, especially under pressure. Strength is the capacity to stand firm in truth, to admit when you need help, and to lead with conviction even when it's uncomfortable. The strongest leaders are not those who never struggle, but those who remain anchored amid storms.

2. Practice Wise Vulnerability
Authenticity does not mean oversharing or being emotionally exposed in every setting. It requires **discernment**—knowing **when, where, and with whom** to be vulnerable. Create trusted spaces where honesty is welcomed and growth is fostered. Wise vulnerability invites collaboration, fosters loyalty, and disarms fear—both in the leader and in those they lead.

3. Resist Isolation
Leadership can be lonely, but it should not be isolating. The myth of the solitary leader is both dangerous and unsustainable. **Surround yourself with community, seek counsel**, and **welcome accountability**. Authentic leadership thrives in relationships where truth is spoken in love and growth is pursued

in unity. Loneliness breeds pride and burnout, but connection fosters humility and resilience.

4. Prioritize Emotional Health
It's easy for leaders to focus solely on results, metrics, and milestones, neglecting their inner world. But emotional health is not optional, it is essential. Invest in self-awareness. Process pain. Make space for rest and renewal. A leader who is emotionally healthy will lead with clarity, compassion, and consistency. Your inner life is not separate from your leadership—it fuels or fractures it.

5. Embrace Grace
No leader is perfect. Every leader is a **work in progress**. Embrace the grace that allows you to lead while still growing, to make mistakes and learn from them, to be human and still worthy of respect. Grace liberates leaders from the impossible burden of perfection and gives them permission to be both bold and broken. Extend grace to yourself and to others—it is the oil that keeps the engine of authentic leadership running.

A New Kind of Leadership
In a world longing for **real connection**, for **honest conversations**, and for **leaders they can trust**, authenticity is the new currency of influence. Leaders who dare to **drop the mask**, to **live whole**, and to **lead with integrity** will not only transform their own leadership, but they will also **liberate others** to live and lead the same way.

Authentic leadership invites people to believe that they, too, can bring their full selves to the table. It builds cultures of trust, fosters creativity, and drives sustainable success. The way forward is not pretending to be more than we are; it's showing up as **all that we are**, with courage, compassion, and conviction.

CHAPTER 9
When Weakness is a Taboo

In many church environments today, an unspoken rule often reigns: *don't look weak*. This cultural norm, though subtle, can be deeply damaging—not only to individuals struggling in silence but also to the entire body of Christ. When weakness is treated as a taboo, we create an environment where masks are worn, struggles are hidden, and healing becomes difficult, if not impossible. Let's explore this through three key lenses:

1. Church Culture and Toxic Perfectionism
The Church was meant to be a refuge for the broken, a hospital for the hurting, and a family for the outcast. At its core, it should reflect the radical grace and mercy of Christ—welcoming sinners, restoring the weary, and creating space for authenticity. Yet, in many modern church cultures, a dangerous distortion has quietly crept into *toxic perfectionism*.

This kind of perfectionism is not the pursuit of excellence or holiness rooted in grace—it's the unhealthy pressure to appear flawless, spiritually accomplished, and always "put together." It creates an environment where external appearance is valued over internal transformation, and where struggles are seen as weaknesses to be hidden, not wounds to be healed.

Instead of fostering a culture of vulnerability, many churches unintentionally reward performance. Testimonies are polished. Leaders are expected to maintain an image of unshakable strength. Congregants often feel the need to wear a spiritual mask, fearing judgment or rejection if they reveal the reality of their inner battles. The unspoken message becomes: *If you're struggling, keep it to yourself. If you're broken, pretend you're not.*

This toxic atmosphere has dire consequences. People silently battle depression, addiction, pornography, marital problems, abuse, and deep doubts about their faith. But instead of finding freedom in confession, they are burdened by shame. Instead of seeking help and healing, they isolate themselves—trapped by the fear of being seen as "less spiritual."

This perfectionism undermines the gospel at its core. The gospel is not about earning God's approval through perfect behavior—it's about receiving His grace in the midst of our imperfections. It declares that *all have sinned and fall short of the glory of God* (Romans 3:23), and that Christ came not for the righteous, but for sinners (Mark 2:17). When the church forgets this, it replaces grace with performance, and discipleship with image management.

Worse still, toxic perfectionism promotes spiritual pride and hypocrisy. It pushes people to compare their righteousness, rather than embrace humility. It creates a culture where repentance is rare and where appearances become more important than actual growth. This not only stunts spiritual maturity but drives people away from genuine community and from Christ Himself.

To counter this culture, churches must intentionally cultivate spaces where honesty is welcomed, and weakness is not shamed but embraced as a gateway to God's power. As Paul reminds us, "*My grace is sufficient for you, for my power is made perfect in weakness"* (2 Corinthians 12:9). We grow by grace, not by pretending.

True revival will not come through perfect performances, but through broken hearts laid bare before God and one another. It will come when pastors can say, "I'm struggling," and congregants can reply, "Me too," without fear. It will flourish when churches are not performance halls, but places where people can come messy—and leave changed by the love of Christ and the support of His body.

The Church must be reminded that God is not glorified by our polished façades, but by our dependence on Him. A culture of grace is not permissive of sin—but it *is* patient with sinners. And only when the Church embodies this grace will it truly reflect the heart of Jesus.

2. Leaders as Humans, Not Gods

In today's church culture, spiritual leaders are often placed on pedestals, seen as untouchable paragons of faith and strength. They are expected to always be right, always be strong, and never show signs of weakness. While honoring our pastors and leaders is both biblical and appropriate— "Let the elders who rule well be considered worthy of double honor" (1 Timothy 5:17)—we veer into dangerous territory when we begin to worship them, even subtly, as flawless oracles rather than as human vessels.

This false expectation of perfection creates a toxic culture, one where leaders feel compelled to wear masks. They cannot admit struggles with doubt, mental health, family issues, or burnout for fear of being seen as unfit for ministry. The result is a leadership that feels isolated, pressured, and often emotionally and spiritually exhausted. Many pastors are suffering silently because their congregation expects them to be invulnerable.

But leaders are not gods. They are not angels. They are not superhumans. They are *humans*, called by God, flawed like everyone else, and deeply in need of grace just like the people they serve. They, too, fight battles in secret. They, too, need safe spaces where they can weep, confess, and be restored. The same grace they preach must also be extended to them. When we expect perfection, we set them up for failure—and when they inevitably falter, we are quick to criticize rather than restore.

A culture that denies leaders the space to be human is a culture that fosters hypocrisy, burnout, and moral failure. We must reimagine our relationship with spiritual authority—not to dishonor, but to humanize. We must learn to hold our leaders up in prayer, not up on pedestals. Pedestals isolate, but community heals. Instead of expecting leaders to carry the weight of perfection, let's offer them a community where honesty is safe and healing is possible.

We desperately need a shift toward a healthier church culture—one where pastors can say, "I'm struggling," or "I need help," without fear of dismissal or disrespect. Vulnerability from leadership is not weakness; it is strength. When a pastor humbly admits their humanity, they are not disqualified from leading—they are demonstrating *how* to lead. In fact, authentic leadership models dependence on Christ, not self.

Moreover, when leaders embrace and model vulnerability, they give permission to the rest of the church to do the same. They show the congregation that it's okay to be in process, that the church is not a museum of saints but a hospital for sinners. This kind of authenticity fosters a healthy, humble, and grace-filled community—one that reflects the heart of Christ, who did not shy away from weakness but bore ours fully.

Let's celebrate our leaders, yes, but let's also protect them by allowing them to be real. Let's champion a culture where confession is not punished, where struggle is not shamed, and where healing is not only preached but practiced—beginning with those who lead us.

3. The Danger of Not Creating Space for Brokenness
When weakness is taboo, brokenness doesn't disappear, it gets buried. And what is buried rarely heals; instead, it festers beneath the surface, silently infecting the soul. In the absence of grace-filled spaces, wounds deepen, hearts harden, and people quietly bleed behind the veil of religion.

The Church was never meant to be a showroom for perfection but a refuge for the hurting. Yet too often, we expect people to clean themselves up before they come in, to fix their lives before they find belonging. But Jesus didn't wait for people to get it together. He sat with sinners, touched lepers, wept with the grieving, and restored the broken. He was moved by compassion, not repelled by imperfection. He didn't shy away from weakness; He entered into it. As Paul reminds us in 2 Corinthians 12:9, *"My grace is sufficient for you, for My power is made perfect in weakness."*

When the Church fails to make room for weakness, it unintentionally nurtures an environment of performance, not transformation. People begin to wear spiritual masks, afraid to admit their struggles, and are ashamed to show their wounds.

Instead of real repentance, they offer polished appearances. Instead of deep healing, they settle for shallow acceptance. They learn to speak in Christian clichés rather than honest prayers.

And the consequences are grave.

When brokenness is buried, sin thrives in the dark. Shame multiplies. Isolation deepens. People suffer silently, believing they are alone in their pain. Marriages crumble, addictions spiral, depression lingers—all while smiles fill the pews and "I'm fine" echoes through the hallways.

A church that refuses to accommodate weakness becomes a breeding ground for pride, performance, and pretension. It becomes a museum of saints rather than a hospital for sinners. But the gospel was never about putting on a good face; it was always about grace meeting us in our worst moments and lifting us into new life.

To reflect Christ, we must be willing to create a culture of vulnerability. We must celebrate honesty, honor the courage it takes to confess, and point each other back to the cross where mercy flows freely. The Church must be a place where people can limp in with their wounds exposed and find healing—not judgment. A place where tears are welcomed, stories are shared, and grace runs deeper than shame.

We must ask ourselves: Do we truly believe in the power of redemption, or do we only applaud the already restored?

If the Church is to be a beacon of hope, it must welcome the broken—not as projects to be fixed, but as people to be loved.

Only then will we see the kind of transformation that turns ashes into beauty, mourning into dancing, and weakness into a platform for God's power.

The body of Christ flourishes not in pretense but in truth. It thrives when we choose honesty over image, vulnerability over performance, and grace over judgment. When we tear down the walls of toxic perfectionism—the pressure to appear flawless and unshakable—we make room for genuine connection, healing, and spiritual growth. The church was never meant to be a museum for the morally elite; it is a hospital for the broken, a refuge for the weary, and a community for the redeemed.

To reclaim our witness and relevance, we must de-idolize our leaders and stop placing them on pedestals they were never meant to stand on. When pastors, ministers, and Christian influencers are allowed to be human—fallible yet faithful—it liberates the entire body to walk in authenticity. Leadership in the Kingdom is not about flawless performance; it's about servant-hearted obedience, humility, and dependence on Christ.

Brokenness is not the antithesis of faith; it is often the very context in which faith becomes most real. Jesus did not come for the righteous, but for sinners. He embraced the leper, wept with the grieving, and restored the fallen. When we embrace our own weaknesses and allow others to do the same, we reflect the heart of Jesus more clearly than a thousand polished sermons ever could.

The church must reclaim its identity as a sanctuary for the struggling—a place where doubts are voiced, wounds are tended, and sin is confronted not with condemnation but with compassion and accountability. This kind of church culture doesn't dilute holiness; it deepens it, because it is rooted in grace and shaped by truth.

Let us normalize weakness, not to glorify failure, but to magnify the strength of our Savior. For His power is made perfect in weakness. When we boast in our insufficiency, we shine a spotlight on His all-sufficiency. Grace becomes visible, love becomes tangible, and Christ becomes central.

May we become a people who do not hide behind masks of spiritual performance but walk freely in the light of God's mercy. Because in a world drowning in comparison, pretense, and pressure, the honest church—the broken but believing church—will be a beacon of hope.

PART FOUR: REDEMPTION IN THE BLEEDING

CHAPTER 10
Leading While Limping

Leadership is often portrayed as strength, charisma, and confidence. But in God's kingdom, leadership is frequently shaped by **limping**—a metaphor for weakness, pain, or imperfection. True leadership is not the absence of wounds, but the willingness to lead *despite* them. The story of **Jacob's limp** (Genesis 32:22–32) serves as a powerful illustration of this truth.

1. Weakness Doesn't Disqualify – Jacob's Limp
Jacob's life had been a series of struggles. From the womb, he was wrestling. First with his brother Esau, then with his father Isaac, then with Laban, and finally, with God Himself. Jacob had always relied on his wits, his words, and his will to manipulate his way through life. But all of that changed at a place called Peniel.

In that defining encounter, Jacob wrestled through the night with what Scripture identifies as a divine being—God Himself. He clung and grappled, determined not to let go without a blessing. And he received it—but not before God touched the socket of his hip and left him permanently limping. From that day on, Jacob—whose name was changed to Israel—would never walk the same again.

But here's the beautiful paradox: Jacob *limped* into his purpose.

His weakness wasn't a mark of shame; it was a sign of transformation. The limp was not evidence of defeat but of a divine encounter. It served as a lasting reminder that Jacob's strength would never again come from self-reliance, manipulation, or natural ability, but from total dependence on God.

And Jacob is not alone.

Throughout Scripture, we see that some of the mightiest men and women God used bore visible or invisible weaknesses—limps of their own:

- **Moses**, the great deliverer, was slow of speech and tongue. His fear of public speaking was so profound that God assigned Aaron to speak on his behalf.
- **Paul**, the apostle who penned much of the New Testament, spoke of a mysterious "thorn in the flesh"—a persistent affliction that kept him humble and dependent on God's grace.
- **David**, the man after God's heart, made devastating moral mistakes and experienced deep family dysfunction. Yet he was still chosen to shepherd a nation and be part of the lineage of Christ.

Their weaknesses didn't disqualify them. They refined them. They redirected their focus away from personal ability and toward God's all-sufficient grace.

In God's kingdom, the limp is often the mark of legitimacy.

We live in a world that celebrates strength, polish, and perfection. But God operates differently. He doesn't seek the flawless; He seeks the surrendered. He doesn't require you to be whole in the eyes of the world—He simply asks you to be yielded in His hands.

So, if you walk with a limp—be it a failure from your past, a weakness in your personality, a limitation in your ability, or a scar from your journey—take heart. God is not trying to erase it; He may be trying to use it.

The limp does not disqualify you. It may, in fact, be the very thing that *qualifies* you.

The world may view weakness as a liability. But in the economy of heaven, weakness becomes the womb of strength.

God told Paul, "My grace is sufficient for you, for My power is made perfect in weakness" (2 Corinthians 12:9). And Paul responded, "Therefore I will boast all the more gladly about my weaknesses, so that Christ's power may rest on me."

Your limp is a testimony. It's a visible sign of an invisible encounter. It says: *I have met God. I have wrestled. I have been broken and blessed. And I walk differently now.*

Let it mark you. Let it humble you. And let it remind you that God does not use perfect people—He perfects the surrendered.

2. Power in Authenticity
We live in a world that rewards image. The louder the platform, the sleeker the presentation, the more applause it seems to gather. Social media thrives on filters and curated moments, leadership often leans toward perfectionism, and public personas are polished until they shine. But beneath the surface, there's a quiet but growing cry—for something deeper, something real. People are not just looking for leaders who impress them; they're looking

for leaders who *connect* with them. And that connection is born not from perfection, but from **authenticity**.

Authentic leadership is not about being flawless; it's about being faithful. It is not about appearing strong at all costs but about having the courage to lead from a place of honesty, vulnerability, and integrity.

The Power of Jacob's Limp

In the Bible, Jacob's story gives us a powerful image of this kind of authenticity. After wrestling with God, Jacob walks away with a limp (Genesis 32:24–31). His limp was not a sign of weakness; it was a **mark of transformation**. He had encountered God. He had wrestled, surrendered, and been changed. His limp was visible—it made him real. He could no longer fake strength; instead, he carried his story openly.

That limp told everyone: *I have struggled. I have failed. But I have also encountered grace. I am not the same.*

When you lead while limping, several powerful things happen:
- **You give others permission to embrace their own struggles.** Your transparency becomes an invitation. You say without words: "You don't have to be perfect to be used by God. You don't have to hide your wounds to walk in purpose."
- **You create trust because people resonate with realness.** People don't follow titles, they follow truth. When others see your authenticity, it lowers their guard. It speaks to the human experience, reminding them they're not alone in their flaws, fears, or failures.

- **You invite God's strength to be perfected in your weakness (2 Corinthians 12:9).** God doesn't ask you to be strong on your own. He simply asks you to show up—and let His power flow through your surrendered life. When we stop pretending and start depending, heaven gets involved.

Authenticity Is Not Oversharing

Let's be clear—authenticity doesn't mean you turn your pain into a public spectacle. It's not an excuse to spill every detail of your private life or to glory in dysfunction. True authenticity is about **alignment**—where your public life reflects your private walk. Where there's no contradiction between what you preach and how you live.

It's about refusing to pretend. It's choosing to be led by grace rather than driven by performance. It's having the humility to say, "I don't have it all together, but I know the One who holds me together."

The Courage to Be Real

In a world that teaches us to market ourselves, being authentic takes courage. But it's the kind of courage that births impact. Because while charisma can draw a crowd, only **character** can build a legacy.

You don't need to hide your limp. You don't need to conceal your scars. In fact, it might be the very thing God uses to reach others. Like Jesus showed Thomas His scars after the resurrection, sometimes our wounds become proof of God's healing, not our failure.

Authentic leaders are not defined by their platform but by their posture—one of humility, surrender, and consistent growth. Don't trade authenticity for applause. The power of your leadership is not in how flawless you appear, but in how faithfully you reflect the grace of God—even when you limp.

3. Purpose in Pain

Jacob's limp was no accident. It wasn't the result of misfortune or carelessness. It was the physical reminder of a divine encounter—an all-night wrestle with God that left him forever changed. His limp marked the moment he stopped striving in his own strength and began to walk under God's authority. It wasn't a sign of weakness; it was the signature of transformation. In God's hands, pain is never purposeless. In fact, it often becomes the very instrument He uses to shape us for greater impact.

In the journey of leadership, pain is inevitable. But in God's economy, *nothing is wasted*—not even your deepest wounds, darkest nights, or most painful failures. They are not setbacks; they are setups for a deeper work within you and through you.

Pain does at least three things in the life of a leader:

1. Refines Character

Pain has a way of stripping away pretense. It reveals what is truly inside of us and brings hidden motives to light. Trials have a refining fire about them—they burn away ego, entitlement, and pride, leaving behind something purer, humbler, and more sincere. A leader who has suffered walks differently—not with arrogance, but with authenticity. Pain tests the heart, and in that testing, character is forged. What remains after the fire is often more usable than what was there before.

2. Births Compassion

The most impactful leaders are often those who limp. Why? Because they've tasted sorrow. They know what it feels like to be broken. And because of that, they lead with empathy instead of judgment, patience instead of pressure, grace instead of criticism. Pain births a tenderness that no classroom or strategy session can impart. Leaders who have been in the valley can guide others through it, not from theory, but from experience. They become safe spaces for the hurting, and voices of hope for the weary.

3. Anchors Dependence

Pain reminds us that we are not God. It dismantles the illusion of control and forces us to our knees. The strongest leaders are not those who lean on their own strength, but those who have learned the secret of leaning on God. Pain becomes a tether that keeps us from drifting into self-reliance. It teaches us to pray again, to listen again, to trust again. It anchors us in the presence and promises of God. And in that place of dependency, we find the strength to keep leading—not from our power, but from His.

If you've walked through hardship—whether physical affliction, emotional wounds, spiritual dryness, or relational betrayals—it does *not* disqualify you. In fact, it may be the very thing that *qualifies* you to lead with deeper authority and greater credibility. Leadership isn't reserved for the flawless. It's entrusted to the faithful. Your scars tell a story, and that story may be the very thing that brings healing to others.

Your limp isn't a liability, it's a legacy.

Let it remind you of your encounter with God. Let it keep you humble, surrendered, and grateful. Let it point others not to your strength, but to *His*. Because in the Kingdom of God, it's often those who limp that lead best—those who have wrestled with God, laid down their pride, and now walk forward with a daily reminder of grace.

So don't hide your limp. Let it speak. Let it testify. Let it lead.

CHAPTER 11
Healing is a Journey, not a Moment

Practical Healing Steps for Leaders
Leadership is demanding—mentally, emotionally, spiritually, and even physically. It often requires pouring into others constantly while receiving little replenishment. When wounds—whether from burnout, betrayal, failure, disappointment, or trauma—occur in the life of a leader, the temptation is to suppress them in favor of "pressing on" for the sake of the people being led. But healing is not a momentary decision or a single event; it is an ongoing journey that demands intentional steps and consistent care.

1. Embrace the Reality of the Wound
The first step in healing is acknowledging that you are hurt. Many leaders' function in denial, hiding behind responsibilities, titles, or busyness. But healing begins when you stop minimizing your pain and start confronting it with honesty. This takes courage but is essential. Naming the wound—be it burnout, betrayal, loss, or moral failure—opens the door to restoration.

2. Pursue Therapy and Professional Help
Therapy is not a sign of weakness; it's a wise investment in your mental and emotional health. Christian or trauma-informed therapy can help leaders unpack deep-seated wounds, unprocessed grief, or patterns of dysfunction that have developed

over time. Counseling provides tools to reframe experiences, develop healthier responses, and rebuild confidence.

3. Prioritize Rest and Rhythms of Renewal
Many leaders break down not because of one overwhelming moment, but because of prolonged neglect of rest. Sleep, solitude, silence, nature, and Sabbath rest are not luxuries—they are lifelines. Creating margin in your life allows your soul to breathe and gives God room to do internal work. Schedule days off, regular breaks, and mini retreats to reset your spirit.

4. Take a Sabbatical When Necessary
There are seasons when regular rest isn't enough. When the wounds are deep or burnout is severe, a sabbatical may be necessary. This extended time away from active leadership allows for physical rejuvenation, spiritual refocus, and emotional recalibration. It's not quitting, it's reloading. Churches and organizations should normalize sabbaticals as a proactive, protective practice for long-term health.

5. Seek Mentorship and Godly Counsel
Every leader needs a voice they trust—someone with wisdom, experience, and compassion who isn't impressed by your platform but is committed to your growth. A mentor helps bring perspective, offers counsel, and walks with you through hard seasons. This relationship is vital for staying grounded and making wise decisions during your healing journey.

6. Establish Accountability Structures
Healing involves walking in the light. Accountability keeps you honest and on track, especially when you're vulnerable. Trusted

friends, elders, or peer leaders who can ask the hard questions and pray with you are essential. Accountability isn't about control; it's about covering. It's a safety net that guards you from self-sabotage and isolation.

7. Learn to Heal While Leading
Sometimes stepping aside isn't immediately possible. Leaders must often heal in motion. This requires a delicate balance—leading with transparency but not bleeding on those you lead. It means giving yourself grace, delegating where needed, and being honest about your limitations. God can use your brokenness as a testimony even as He's still mending you. The goal isn't to pretend you're whole—it's to lead authentically while journeying toward wholeness.

8. Stay Connected to God
Above all, healing is incomplete without intimacy with God. Time in the Word, worship, prayer, and simply being still before Him are not optional during the healing process, they are the essence of it. God is not only the Great Physician; He is your Father, Comforter, and Strength. Let Him minister to your inner wounds. He knows how to restore the soul of a weary shepherd.

Healing is not a checkbox; it is a continual unfolding—a sacred process of becoming whole again. For leaders, it's not a luxury but a necessity. You cannot give what you don't have. Prioritize your health. Embrace your journey. And remember, even as you serve others, God is serving you—mending what was broken and refilling what was empty. One step at a time.

CHAPTER 12
The Ultimate Bleeding Leader

In a world that often defines leadership by dominance, charisma, and power, Jesus Christ stands as the ultimate contradiction — the **Bleeding Leader**, whose strength was revealed not in conquest, but in crucifixion. His leadership was not about demanding allegiance but about laying down His life for those He led. It was not a throne of gold, but a cross of wood stained with blood. Christ's example redefines what it means to lead: to suffer, to intercede, and to redeem.

1. Christ: Perfect Example of Leadership Through Suffering
True leadership is not measured by crowns, applause, or titles, but by scars — and no one embodies this better than Jesus Christ. His path to glory was not through earthly power or dominance, but through suffering, sacrifice, and self-emptying love. At the center of Christian leadership stands a cross, not a throne.

Jesus Christ, though eternally God, did not cling to His divine privileges. As Philippians 2:5–8 declares, *"Let this mind be in you which was also in Christ Jesus, who, being in the form of God, thought it not robbery to be equal with God, but made Himself of no reputation, and took upon Him the form of a servant... and became obedient unto death, even the death of the cross."* This passage presents a radical model of leadership — not grasping for power but letting go of it for the sake of others.

Instead of leading with force, He led with a towel around His waist, stooping low to wash the feet of those who would soon abandon Him. He didn't demand service; He gave it. He didn't command from a distance; He entered the mess, touched the untouchables, embraced the broken, and healed the marginalized. He walked beside the rejected, mourned with the sorrowful, and welcomed sinners with open arms. His leadership was deeply personal, profoundly compassionate, and undeniably costly.

In Gethsemane, we see perhaps the clearest picture of His inner battle—*"Father, if it be possible, let this cup pass from Me. Yet not My will, but Yours be done."* (Matthew 26:39). The weight of humanity's sin bore down on Him, yet He chose obedience. He did not sidestep the suffering. He did not seek comfort. He chose the cross—not for Himself, but for the redemption of others. This is the essence of servant leadership: laying down one's life so others might live.

Christ endured betrayal by a friend, denial by a disciple, injustice from religious leaders, and brutality from soldiers. He bore mockery, thorns, nails, and finally, the silence of the Father as He hung between heaven and earth. And through it all, He loved. *"Father, forgive them,"* He cried, even as they crucified Him. That is leadership—choosing love in the face of hate, mercy in the face of cruelty, and faithfulness in the face of unimaginable suffering.

By embracing the cross, Jesus turned the world's idea of leadership upside down. He taught that real leaders don't use people to climb ladders; they carry others on their backs. They don't run from pain—they walk through it, trusting that God will redeem it. They bleed, not for praise, but for purpose.

The resurrected Christ still bears the scars in His hands and side — not as marks of defeat, but as eternal reminders that true leadership leaves a mark, and that pain, when surrendered to God, becomes the path to glory.

Leadership through suffering means embracing hardship not as a curse, but as a calling. It means being willing to suffer for what is right, to endure for the good of others, and to walk humbly with God even when the cost is high. The world may not applaud this kind of leadership, but heaven recognizes and honors it.

So, let Christ be our model—not just in His miracles, but in His suffering. Let His humility shape our ambition. Let His obedience guide our decisions. And let His love—even unto death—become the heartbeat of our leadership.

2. Bleeding But Still Interceding

Even in His most agonizing moments, Jesus Christ did not fall silent. Suspended between earth and heaven, nailed to a cross, bruised and bloodied beyond recognition, His voice did not curse, complain, or condemn. Instead, it carried compassion. His words were not of vengeance but of mercy: *"Father, forgive them, for they know not what they do"* (Luke 23:34). He was bleeding yet still interceding.

This is the portrait of divine leadership—raw, real, and redemptive. It's easy to pray when life is comfortable, to speak kindly when we are treated well, to show grace when things go according to plan. But Christ demonstrated something greater. At the peak of His pain, He carried the weight of humanity's sin and still had room in His heart to plead for our forgiveness. This is not just empathy; it is sacrificial advocacy. He did not wait for

His wounds to close before He began to pray—His prayers poured out even as His blood did.

To intercede while bleeding is to lead with a love that transcends personal suffering. It is to stand in the gap for others even while you're being crushed. It is to carry burdens that are not yours, to lift others when you're barely standing. This is what Jesus modeled on the cross—a leadership and love that bleeds but does not break.

His intercession was not passive; it was powerful. Every drop of blood shed was not a sign of defeat but a seal of redemption. His wounds weren't just symbols of suffering; they were keys to salvation. The cross did not conquer Christ—Christ conquered through the cross.

And the miracle is that He has never stopped interceding.

Hebrews 7:25 declares, *"Therefore He is able to save completely those who come to God through Him, because He always lives to intercede for them."* Jesus is still the Intercessor. Though no longer bleeding, He still bears the scars—eternal reminders of His love and sacrifice. Those nail-pierced hands now stretch out in glory, still lifted in intercession for you and me. He doesn't forget us. He doesn't stop advocating. His ministry did not end at the resurrection—it continues at the right hand of the Father.

To follow Christ, then, is to lead like Him. It means we must learn to pray even while we bleed, to serve even when we suffer, to forgive even when we've been betrayed. True leadership is not measured by how high we climb, but by how deeply we bleed for the sake of others—and still choose to intercede.

When you're misunderstood, keep praying. When you're wounded by those you love, keep forgiving. When life feels heavy and unfair, keep standing in the gap.

Bleeding does not disqualify you from intercession. In fact, it may be the very thing that makes your intercession more powerful—because it flows not just from your lips, but from your life.

So, like Christ, let your trials become altars. Let your wounds become testimonies. Let your intercession become a lifeline for those too weak to pray for themselves.

Bleed if you must—but never stop interceding.

3. The Redemptive Value of Suffering

In the kingdom of God, suffering is never wasted. Unlike the world, which sees suffering as weakness, failure, or misfortune, Scripture reveals a divine paradox: in Christ, suffering is often the very soil in which redemption grows. The cross of Christ stands as the ultimate testimony that God can take what is broken, bloody, and despised—and use it to save the world.

"He was pierced for our transgressions, He was crushed for our iniquities; the punishment that brought us peace was on Him, and by His wounds we are healed" (Isaiah 53:5).

These are not poetic words only; they are prophetic declarations of the redemptive mystery of God. Christ's wounds were not in vain—they were the instruments of our healing. His suffering was not a detour in the plan of God; it *was* the plan. What looked like defeat became the doorway to eternal victory. What the world saw as shame, God turned into salvation. The blood-stained cross, once a symbol of terror and execution, has become the throne of grace and the emblem of eternal hope.

Suffering as a Tool in the Life of the Believer

This same principle carries over into the lives of those who follow Christ. For the believer—and especially for the Christian leader—suffering is not a sign of God's absence, but often of His active shaping. Trials do not mean disqualification; they are often preparation. Pain does not always signify punishment; it can be the path to purpose.

God uses suffering to:
- **Refine character** – Like gold in the fire, our true selves are purified through affliction.
- **Deepen empathy** – We are made tender toward others when we have walked through sorrow ourselves.
- **Strip away pride** – Pain humbles us, reminding us of our dependence on God.
- **Strengthen faith** – In weakness, we discover the strength that only comes from Christ.
- **Increase authority** – True spiritual authority is often born not in ease, but in endurance.

In the hands of God, our tears become tools, our burdens become bridges, and our scars become sacred.

The Bleeding Leader

Jesus, the **Ultimate Bleeding Leader**, did not ascend to power through dominance, but through sacrifice. His leadership looked nothing like Caesar's throne or Herod's palace. His crown was woven from thorns, not gold. His robe was soaked in blood, not royal perfume. His exaltation came not through applause, but through crucifixion.

He redefined what it means to lead. He taught that the greatest among us must become the servant of all — and not just in service, but often in suffering. The Bleeding Leader shows us that leadership in God's kingdom flows from woundedness, not mere giftedness. His blood led the greatest exodus in history — not from a physical empire, but from the bondage of sin and death.

Your Wounds Can Water Others
To follow in the footsteps of the Bleeding Leader is to understand that your own suffering can become a source of strength for others. Your scars can speak more loudly than your sermons. Your pain, when placed in God's hands, becomes a platform for healing. Just as Christ's blood birthed a church, your trials—surrendered, not suppressed—can birth transformation in those you lead.

Paul said in 2 Corinthians 4:10, *"We always carry around in our body the death of Jesus, so that the life of Jesus may also be revealed in our body."* Our dying — to pride, to comfort, to convenience—often becomes the channel through which the life of Christ is made visible.

Leaders who bleed like Christ become fountains of grace for a broken world. Their leadership is not sanitized or scripted but soaked in authenticity and anchored in the crucified life.

Embracing the Cross
To be a leader after Christ's heart is to embrace the cross, not evade it. It is to:

- **S**erve while suffering.
- Intercede while wounded.
- Love while bleeding.
- Hope while hurting.

It is believed that in God's economy, *brokenness is not a barrier to leadership—it is often the very badge of it.*

The world teaches us to lead from strength, from image, from success. But Christ calls us to lead from the cross. And that is the hardest, yet holiest kind of leadership.

So, are you willing to lead like Christ—not from a place of ease, but through the power of redemptive sacrifice?

Will you let your wounds speak? Will you allow your pain to produce fruit in others? Will you trust that what breaks you today may build someone else tomorrow?

In Christ, even bleeding is beautiful—when it is poured out in love.

PART FIVE: PRACTICAL TOOLS FOR WOUNDED LEADERS

CHAPTER 13
Safe Spaces and Safe People

In a world filled with pressure, noise, and emotional complexity, having safe spaces and safe people is not just a luxury; it's a necessity. Whether you're navigating personal challenges, spiritual growth, emotional healing, or simply trying to live with authenticity and purpose, your environment and the people around you play a powerful role in shaping your journey. Safe spaces and safe people help you flourish, heal, and grow. They provide emotional refuge, offer wise counsel, and foster a sense of belonging that is essential for wholeness.

Building a Trusted Circle
In life, storms are inevitable—emotional, spiritual, or relational. During such times, having a *trusted circle* isn't just beneficial, it's essential. A trusted circle is not a crowd; it is a carefully chosen few who walk with you not because of what you offer, but because of who you are. These individuals are emotionally mature, spiritually anchored, and genuinely committed to your well-being. They don't see your scars as stains, they see them as stories, and they honor your journey without judgment.

The Nature of a Trusted Circle
A trusted circle isn't about popularity or proximity. It's not just family or long-time friends; it's about *alignment*. Alignment in values, in truth, in accountability, and in spiritual purpose. These

people are not perfect—but they are safe, stable, and sincere. They bring wisdom without arrogance, presence without pressure, and truth without condemnation.

Characteristics to Look For
Building this kind of circle takes **discernment, intentionality,** and **vulnerability.** Look for individuals who consistently demonstrate the following:
- **Confidentiality:** They don't use your pain as punchlines or prayer gossip. They can be trusted with your raw moments and won't weaponize your weaknesses.
- **Truth in Love:** They speak with honesty, not flattery. They won't tell you what you *want* to hear, but what you *need* to hear—wrapped in love and respect.
- **Challenge with Acceptance:** They push you toward growth but don't shame you for where you are. They see your potential while respecting your present process.
- **Respect for Boundaries:** They understand when to step in and when to give space. They don't suffocate you or take offense when you need solitude.
- **Spiritual Support:** They intercede for you when you're too weak to pray. They lift you up spiritually, standing with you in faith and reminding you of God's promises.

Why It Matters?
When life becomes heavy, these relationships act as anchors. They keep you grounded when emotions threaten to drift you away. They become your:
- Mirrors – helping you see clearly when your perspective is clouded.
- Truth-Tellers – confronting lies you may believe about

yourself or your situation.
- **Cheerleaders** – celebrating your victories, however small, and encouraging you to press on.
- **Intercessors** – covering you in prayer when your own voice is silenced by pain.

The Process Takes Time

A trusted circle is cultivated, not collected. It is not formed overnight. It takes:
- **Time** to observe character.
- **Discernment** to choose wisely.
- **Consistency** to deepen trust.
- **Vulnerability** to let others in.

Not everyone can or should be part of your inner circle. Protect your space. Give your trust carefully but generously to those who earn it. And remember, being part of someone else's trusted circle is also a calling—be the kind of friend you're seeking.

Finding a Mentor, Counselor, or Spiritual Director

There comes a point in every person's journey where the support of friends or peers is no longer enough. While community is vital, there are seasons when the complexities of life—whether emotional, spiritual, or personal- require a deeper level of guidance and support. This is where mentors, counselors, and spiritual directors come in. These individuals are not just helpers; they are companions on the path of growth, healing, and transformation. Each serves a distinct yet equally important role in shaping who you are becoming.

Mentor: The Voice of Experience and Wisdom

A mentor is someone who walks ahead of you in a particular area of life—be it career, relationships, personal development, or faith—and reaches back to offer guidance. They've navigated the terrain you are currently walking through. Mentors do not pretend to have all the answers, but they carry the wisdom of hindsight. Their insight can help you avoid unnecessary pitfalls, identify blind spots, and pursue your purpose with greater clarity. Mentorship often blossoms into a meaningful relationship where your growth is encouraged, your dreams are refined, and your values are affirmed.

A good mentor listens, challenges, encourages, and sometimes even corrects in love. They help you stretch beyond your comfort zone without losing your identity. Finding a mentor may involve seeking out someone whose life bears the kind of fruit you admire, someone whose journey inspires you not just by what they've achieved, but by how they live.

Counselor: The Healer of Wounds and Guide to Wholeness
While mentors offer guidance through experience, counselors are professionally trained to walk with you through the inner workings of the heart and mind. Life inevitably leaves us with scars—childhood wounds, relational trauma, anxiety, grief, identity struggles, or unresolved pain. A counselor provides a safe, confidential space to unpack those layers without shame or fear of judgment.

They help you make sense of your story, recognize destructive patterns, and develop healthier emotional tools. Whether you're battling depression, coping with loss, trying to navigate family dysfunction, or just needing help to manage stress, seeking a counselor is not a sign of weakness; it is an act of strength and courage. Healing often begins when you stop pretending everything is fine and start addressing what's really going on.

Spiritual Director: The Companion for the Soul

In a noisy world full of distractions and demands, spiritual direction offers a sacred space to pause and listen for the voice of God. A spiritual director is not there to fix you or give you a formula. Instead, they help you become more aware of God's movement in your everyday life. Through prayer, silence, Scripture, and spiritual reflection, they guide you toward deeper discernment and intimacy with God.

Whether you're seeking clarity in a major decision, wrestling with doubt, or longing to experience God's presence more fully, a spiritual director walks with you in that journey. They ask meaningful questions that draw you closer to your soul's deepest desires and God's unique call on your life. Spiritual direction is about awakening—not achievement.

Why Seeking Help Is Not a Weakness

In a culture that often glorifies independence and self-reliance, it's easy to believe the lie that asking for help is a form of failure. But nothing could be further from the truth. Just as you wouldn't hesitate to visit a doctor when your body is in pain, you shouldn't delay seeking help for emotional or spiritual pain. Taking your inner well-being seriously is not a weakness; it's wisdom.

Even the strongest people need support. In fact, strength is often defined not by how much you can carry alone, but by your willingness to lean on others when the load gets too heavy. Whether through a mentor's insight, a counselor's care, or a spiritual director's discernment, help is available—and it's worth seeking.

You Don't Have to Do Life Alone
There is no shame in needing guidance. Life is complex, and navigating it well often requires the humility to say, "I need help." The people who grow the most, heal the deepest, and live the fullest are those who are willing to reach out.

So, if you feel stuck, confused, overwhelmed, or spiritually dry, take the step. Seek a mentor. Book that counseling session. Reach out to a spiritual director. Your future self will thank you for the courage you showed today.

Safe spaces and safe people are not luxuries—they are necessities for the healing and flourishing of the human soul. They create the emotional and spiritual soil where wounds can be gently tended, scars can become stories, and growth can take root. In a world that often wounds and rushes, sacred spaces—whether physical or relational—offer the rare gift of rest, reflection, and restoration.

Do not underestimate the profound power of wise companionship. The presence of people who genuinely care, who speak truth in love, and who offer grace without condition can be life-altering. These are the people who see the mess and still choose to stay, who challenge you to grow without crushing your spirit, and who remind you of your worth when you forget it yourself.

Healing does not happen in isolation. It happens in the context of relationships—relationships where you are seen, heard, and valued. That's why it is so important to *build your circle* with intention. Surround yourself with those who reflect the heart of God, those who carry light into your darkest places, and those who hold your heart with tenderness and integrity.

Seek guidance. There is no shame in admitting you need help; there is wisdom in knowing you cannot do life alone. Lean into mentors, counselors, spiritual leaders, and mature friends who can speak into your journey with insight and compassion.

Be intentional. Safe spaces rarely happen by accident. They are built on boundaries, trust, prayer, and discernment. Be deliberate about who you let into your life and where you plant your soul. Choose environments that nurture truth, foster growth, and reflect God's grace.

Because healing happens best—not in noise, not in judgment, not in striving—but in places where love dwells, truth is honored, and grace is abundant. That's where the soul breathes freely. That's where transformation begins.

CHAPTER 14
Boundaries and Balance

In a fast-paced world that constantly demands more from us—emotionally, physically, and spiritually—setting clear boundaries and maintaining a healthy balance is essential for long-term well-being and fruitful relationships. Boundaries are not walls to isolate, but fences to protect what matters most. Balance is not about equal distribution, but about wise and intentional prioritization. Below are key principles that help establish both:

1. Learning to Say No
Saying "no" is often misunderstood. In many cultures and personal upbringings, we're conditioned to associate "no" with rejection, rebellion, or selfishness. But in truth, learning to say "no" is a sign of *maturity*, *clarity*, and *inner strength*. It's not about closing doors for others—it's about opening the right doors for yourself.

Many people live in a cycle of constant overcommitment because they fear disappointing others, being seen as unkind, or losing opportunities. However, when we always say "yes" to everyone and everything, we slowly say "no" to the very things that matter most: our peace of mind, our health, our relationships, and our purpose. Your time and energy are not infinite; they are precious resources given by God to be used wisely.

Saying "no" is not rejection—it is redirection.

It is you choosing what deserves your *best* attention, rather than spreading yourself thin over things that only drain you. Jesus Himself often withdrew from the crowds to rest and pray. He didn't heal every person in every town. He knew His mission and stayed focused on it, modeling healthy boundaries even in ministry.

Why Saying "No" Matters:
- **Protects your time and energy:** Time is one thing you can never get back. Saying "no" helps you use your time with intention.
- **Preserves your mental and emotional health:** Overextending leads to burnout, resentment, and anxiety. Boundaries are a form of self-care.
- **Prioritizes your God-given assignment:** You were not created to please everyone—you were created to fulfill a purpose.
- **Strengthens your relationships:** People who respect your boundaries are the ones you can build deeper trust with. Saying "no" filters out relationships built on guilt or obligation.

How to Say No Graciously:
You can say "no" without being rude, cold, or dismissive. Here's how:
- **Be honest but kind:** *"Thank you for thinking of me, but I won't be able to commit to this right now."*
- Offer alternatives only if you want to: *"I can't take this on, but perhaps you could ask [another person]?"*
- Avoid over-explaining: A clear and simple "no" is better than a long-winded excuse.

- Say it with confidence and peace: Don't apologize for honoring your priorities.

Practical Tip:
Before you say "yes" to any new request, pause. Ask yourself:
1. Does this align with my values and priorities?
2. Do I have the emotional and physical capacity to take this on without harming my peace?
3. Will saying "yes" help or hinder the things God has placed in my hands right now?

If the answer is no, then your response should be a loving, confident "no"—with no guilt attached. Remember, your "no" to one thing is a "yes" to something better.

Saying "no" is not about being hard—it's about being wise. It's how you protect your peace, preserve your purpose, and honor the boundaries that keep your life healthy and fruitful. **Don't be afraid to say "no"—be afraid of living a life disconnected from what truly matters.**

2. Delegation and Trust
You were never meant to carry every load alone. No matter how gifted, anointed, or capable you are, trying to do everything by yourself is neither sustainable nor scriptural. Whether in ministry, family, work, or leadership, effective delegation is not a sign of weakness—it is a mark of maturity, wisdom, and trust in God's design for community.

In Exodus 18, Moses learned this firsthand when his father-in-law Jethro observed him judging the people from morning till evening. Jethro wisely advised him to appoint capable men to share the load. Moses could have resisted, thinking he was the only one fit to lead. Instead, he humbly accepted the counsel and delegated responsibility, which brought relief to him and better service to the people.

Delegation allows others to rise and shine in their unique giftings. It's not just about reducing your burden—it's about increasing capacity in the team and releasing potential in others. It communicates, *"I trust you. I believe in you. Your contribution matters."* This cultivates ownership, accountability, and growth, both in individuals and in the organization.

Trusting others with responsibility is also an act of humility. It says, *"I am not the savior. I am part of a body."* It frees you from the trap of control and perfectionism—two imposters that often dress up as diligence but lead to exhaustion, frustration, and resentment. You were never meant to be everywhere, do everything, and fix everyone. Only God can carry that weight.

In leadership, micromanagement stifles innovation and diminishes morale. On the other hand, healthy delegation fosters collaboration, team spirit, and mutual respect. It communicates value and gives people room to learn, fail, improve, and thrive. Remember: trust is not given blindly but built gradually. People may not do things exactly the way you would, but different doesn't mean wrong. Let go of the need for perfection and embrace the process of growth.

Practical Tip:
Start small. Identify tasks or roles that can be shared or reassigned. Don't just dump work—**equip** and **empower** others with clear expectations, training, and encouragement. Stay available for

guidance but avoid hovering. Allow space for learning curves and be patient with mistakes. Celebrate progress, however small. Building trust takes time, but the reward is a stronger, healthier team—and a more balanced you.

3. Sabbath and Self-Care as non-negotiables

In a world that celebrates hustle and applauds constant productivity, it's easy to fall into the trap of measuring our worth by our output. But God, in His infinite wisdom, designed a rhythm for our lives that includes intentional pauses. The Sabbath was not instituted for God's benefit—it was given for ours. From the very beginning, God modeled rest after creation, not because He was tired, but because He was setting an example for us to follow. This principle isn't about legalism; it's about grace, balance, and trust.

Sabbath: A Divine Invitation to Pause

Sabbath is more than just a day off work. It's a holy invitation to cease striving and recognize that the world doesn't revolve around us. It is a weekly reminder that our identity is not in what we do but in who we are in Christ. When we ignore this sacred rhythm, we suffer the consequences: stress, burnout, confusion, and a loss of spiritual sensitivity.

Observing the Sabbath isn't about checking a religious box. It's about aligning with God's pattern for sustainable living. It's an act of faith to stop and rest, trusting that God will take care of what we leave unfinished. It allows room for reflection, prayer, worship, and connection with loved ones. It rejuvenates us so we can return to our responsibilities with clarity and purpose.

Self-Care: Sacred Stewardship
Self-care is often misunderstood in Christian circles as selfish or worldly, but at its core, self-care is about stewardship. Your body is the temple of the Holy Spirit (1 Corinthians 6:19-20), and taking care of it is an act of worship. When we ignore our physical, emotional, or mental needs, we short-circuit our ability to serve others effectively. You can't pour from an empty cup.

Self-care isn't about expensive spa days or isolation from responsibility. It's about intentionally nurturing your inner and outer life—spending time in the Word, getting adequate sleep, fueling your body with nutritious food, exercising, processing your emotions, and doing things that bring joy and peace. When you take time to tend to your needs in a God-honoring way, you reflect the care and order of your Creator.

Why These Must Be Non-Negotiables
When Sabbath and self-care become optional, they eventually disappear. And when they disappear, you begin to live on fumes—spiritually drained, emotionally unstable, and physically exhausted. But when they become non-negotiables, you live from a place of abundance. You lead better, love deeper, and serve longer.

Making space for rest is not a weakness—it's wisdom. Setting boundaries around your energy, time, and emotional health is not selfish; it's necessary for longevity in your calling. Jesus Himself withdrew from the crowds to pray and recharge (Luke 5:16). If the Son of God needed solitude and rest, how much more do we?

Practical Tips for Embracing Rest and Self-Care

- **Schedule Sabbath intentionally**: Block out time weekly—whether it's a full day or set hours—for rest, worship, and activities that bring peace and joy. Turn off work notifications, resist the urge to "catch up," and lean into God's rest.
- **Start each day with stillness**: Begin your mornings with silence, Scripture, and prayer to center your soul before engaging the world.
- **Move your body regularly**: Exercise is not just physical; it boosts your emotional well-being and mental clarity.
- **Fuel your body with nourishment**: What you eat affects how you feel. Choose food that energizes and heals.
- **Guard your mind**: Limit negativity and chaos. Protect your thought life with truth, gratitude, and positive input.
- **Find moments of joy**: Laugh, play, explore, and connect with nature. Let your heart breathe.
- **Set boundaries**: Learn to say no without guilt so you can say yes to what truly matters.

Let rest and self-care become acts of worship in your daily and weekly rhythm. When you honor God with your whole being—body, mind, and spirit—you become a vessel ready to be filled and poured out again and again.

You cannot pour into others from an empty vessel. No matter how sincere your intentions or how deeply you care, when your mind, body, and spirit are drained, your ability to love, serve, and connect becomes diminished. This is why setting boundaries and maintaining balance are not acts of selfishness; they are acts of stewardship. When you protect your time, energy, and emotional well-being, you're not shutting people out; you're choosing to show up for them with your full presence, undivided attention, and a heart that is whole and replenished.

Living aligned with God's design means honoring the rhythms of rest, renewal, and responsibility. Jesus Himself often withdrew from the crowds to pray and reconnect with the Father—not to escape, but to refuel so He could continue to fulfill His purpose with clarity and strength. In the same way, you are called to live with intentionality, choosing rest over restlessness and stillness over striving. Choose clarity over guilt—the kind that manipulates you into overextending yourself—and health over hustle, which glorifies exhaustion as a badge of honor.

Remember, balance is not about perfection; it's about discernment. It's the wisdom to know what to say yes to, what to say no to, and when to pause and be still. It's the grace to recognize your limitations and the courage to honor them. As you embrace this, you'll discover that giving your best to others is only possible when you are first rooted in wholeness, grounded in peace, and surrendered to God's divine order for your life.

CHAPTER 15
Leading with Scars, Not Open Wounds

Leadership born out of pain can be powerful, but it must come from a place of healing, not raw hurt. While wounds demand attention, scars tell stories. They are reminders of battles fought, lessons learned, and strength developed. A leader who leads with scars—not open wounds—has taken time to process pain, extract wisdom, and emerge with clarity and empathy, not bitterness or unresolved trauma.

Learning When to Step Back
One of the greatest acts of maturity is recognizing the moment to pause, to pull back, and to breathe. Life will inevitably bring seasons of emotional pain, betrayal, failure, and trauma. These experiences, while part of the human journey, can cloud judgment, skew motives, and trigger unhealthy reactions. In such moments, trying to lead, serve, or persist as if nothing happened can do more harm than good. It's like trying to navigate a storm with a broken compass—your direction will be off, and those who follow you may be led astray.

Stepping back is not a sign of weakness. It is a bold, wise, and courageous decision. It is the awareness that your soul needs tending, your mind needs rest, and your heart needs healing. It is giving yourself permission to not be okay for a while, so you can become whole again. Pausing doesn't mean you're giving up, it means you're refueling, reorienting, and restoring what life or leadership may have depleted.

When we are wounded, especially in leadership or relationships, we risk bleeding on those who never cut us. Unhealed wounds can make us harsh, reactive, suspicious, or emotionally unavailable. Without realizing it, we begin to speak from pain rather than wisdom, act from trauma rather than truth, and make decisions based on fear rather than faith.

Taking a step back creates room for healing—through self-reflection, therapy, prayer, journaling, solitude, and meaningful conversations. It helps to reframe your identity, not by what you do, but by who you are becoming. It is a sacred season where God often whispers the loudest, reminding you that your value is not found in performance, productivity, or public image, but in your personhood.

This decision is not just for your sake—it's an act of love toward others. When you retreat to heal, you protect those you serve from the backlash of your inner turmoil. You give yourself the chance to return—not bitter or broken, but better. With fresh perspective, grounded strength, and renewed clarity, you can re-engage your purpose with wisdom, compassion, and authenticity.

So, if you find yourself weary, emotionally drained, spiritually dry, or mentally scattered, give yourself permission to pause. Say no without guilt. Step back without shame. Let the world spin without your constant involvement for a while. The truth is, nothing truly healthy grows from a place of burnout. But much can flourish from a place of restoration.

In the end, knowing when to step back is not abandonment of duty—it's stewardship of destiny.

Lessons from the Wound

Every wound carries a lesson, but it takes courage to sit with the pain long enough to receive it. In a culture that glorifies instant healing and quick fixes, it's tempting to patch things up and move on. But when we bypass pain, we also bypass the growth it brings. Wounds—whether from broken relationships, betrayal, deep loss, disappointment, or personal failure—are not just interruptions in our lives; they are invitations to transformation.

Pain has a way of peeling back the layers we use to cover our true selves. It exposes the places we tried to hide, the illusions we clung to, and the expectations we set too high. It shows us where we depended too much on people, outcomes, or status for our sense of identity and worth. When we allow ourselves to truly feel the sting of the wound without rushing to numb it or explain it away, we enter a sacred space of learning.

The wound becomes a classroom. In its quiet, aching moments, we start to hear our own voice more clearly. We begin to discover our limits—not as weaknesses, but as boundaries that protect our wholeness. We become more acquainted with our core values, recognizing what truly matters and what no longer deserves our energy. Some wounds even help us discern our deeper calling, refining our purpose through fire and friction.

We also learn how to hold space for others. When you've known the crushing weight of sorrow or the slow burn of betrayal, you become gentler with others in their suffering. You no longer rush to fix things with hollow words or oversimplified advice. Instead, you offer presence. You learn that empathy often sounds like silence, and compassion can simply be sitting beside someone in their darkness without needing to light a candle too soon.

Over time, these lessons become more than personal insights—they form the bedrock of character. They become the foundation upon which empathy, resilience, and wisdom are built. They turn your wounds into wisdom and your scars into signposts for others. You learn to lead not from a place of perfection, but from a place of understanding. You recognize that your healing journey equips you to guide others, not as someone who has all the answers, but as someone who knows the questions that matter.

The wound may never fully disappear. But it will change you—and if you let it, it will change you for the better.

Using Your Pain to Serve Others Wisely
Pain, when fully processed and healed, is not just a reminder of suffering but a vessel of wisdom, empathy, and strength. It becomes more than a memory—it becomes a ministry. When you've walked through valleys, climbed out of pits, and endured seasons of darkness, your scars become sacred testimonies. They mark not just survival but transformation. And once healed, you can begin to serve others—not from a place of brokenness, but from the clarity, strength, and grace that healing brings.

Scars as Roadmaps, Not Open Wounds
When you are still bleeding, it's hard to offer clean hands to help others. But when the wound has closed and turned into a scar, it becomes a powerful map. It shows where you've been, what you've learned, and how to guide others through the terrain

you've already crossed. Scars don't speak of shame; they speak of survival. They quietly say, *"You're not alone. I've been there too."*

But wise service means waiting until your heart is no longer driven by a need for attention, pity, or validation. It's dangerous to try to lead others when you're still seeking healing yourself. In that state, you're more likely to confuse empathy with projection, and service with self-soothing. True service is birthed from wholeness, not desperation.

Serving with Discernment and Grace
Using your story wisely means being discerning. Not every detail needs to be shared, not every lesson needs to be told. There is a time to speak and a time to stay silent. There's wisdom in knowing the difference. Every space isn't a stage. Every audience doesn't need your autobiography.

Wise servants don't hijack moments to relive their own pain. They don't turn every mentoring session into a confessional. Instead, they use their experience to *listen deeply*, to *empathize authentically*, and to *respond humbly*. Sometimes the greatest act of service is to say nothing—just to sit with someone in their pain, offering presence instead of solutions.

Pain as Preparation for Purpose
Healed pain gives you eyes to see what others might miss—emotional warning signs, spiritual exhaustion, silent cries for help. You recognize the signs of burnout, trauma, or self-sabotage because you once wore those very signs yourself. Your journey equips you to lovingly intervene, to speak life, and to offer guidance without arrogance or assumption.

This kind of service isn't reactive. It's redemptive. It's not about spotlighting yourself; it's about spotlighting *hope*. You don't point people to your story—you point them through your story to the God who heals, the strength that restores, and the truth that sets free.

Lead with Scars, Not Wounds
There is power in scars. They don't hide the past, but neither do they dominate the present. They remind you—and those you serve—that healing *is* possible. That broken things *can* be restored. That God wastes *nothing*.

But you must not rush the process. Don't hurry to lead from a place that hasn't yet been redeemed. Leading from a wound risks bleeding on those you're trying to help. Let God finish His work in you. Let the wound close. Let the scar form. Then, and only then, step forward in service.

Let your scars tell stories—not of bitterness, not of shame—but of redemption, resilience, and revival. Serve with wisdom. Speak with humility. Love with gentleness. And remember, sometimes your greatest ministry isn't what you say, but the quiet courage of simply showing up as someone who has healed.

CHAPTER 16
Beauty from Bleeding

Pain has a way of feeling final, overwhelming, and isolating—but the truth is, it is often the very soil in which beauty grows. When we talk about "beauty from bleeding," we are acknowledging that the seasons of wounding, heartbreak, and hardship are not wasted in God's hands. Rather, they become the very material from which He writes redemption stories.

Summary and Encouragement
As we reflect on the journey of bleeding and healing, it's vital to understand that pain is not the end of your story—it's part of a greater narrative of restoration and redemption. Life wounds us in many ways: through emotional trauma, betrayal, heartbreak, disappointment, rejection, or even the silent weight of grief. But even in the bleeding, there is purpose. Even in the brokenness, there is a whisper of hope.

God never wastes pain. Every tear you've cried, every sleepless night, every moment you felt like giving up—He sees it all. The wounds you carry are not signs of weakness; they are invitations. Invitations for God to enter the deepest parts of your soul, to bring healing where you hurt, and to transform what the enemy meant for evil into a testimony of grace.

Sometimes, healing doesn't come all at once. It is a journey—sometimes slow, sometimes painful—but always sacred. The bleeding is often where God begins His most powerful work. Those places you want to hide are the very places He wants to touch. Where you see a scar, God sees a story. Where you see brokenness, He sees beauty in the making.

Your scars are not a source of shame; they are proof that you survived. They are reminders that you walked through fire but were not consumed. That you faced battles but did not lose your faith. That God's hand was on you, even when you couldn't feel it.

So be encouraged. You may feel weak now, but strength is rising. You may feel shattered, but you are being reshaped. The cracks in your soul are not your ruin—they are the very places where His light is pouring in. Don't be afraid of your healing process. Don't rush it. God is doing something in you that will echo beyond your lifetime.

Hold on to this truth: **your bleeding is not in vain**. Every step you take, every breath you muster, every time you choose to hope again—heaven celebrates your courage. Keep going. The God who allowed the bleeding is the same God who brings the balm. The same hands that were nailed to the cross now hold you close.

You are not alone. You are not forgotten. And you are not finished.

There is more ahead for you. There is purpose beyond the pain. Keep trusting. Keep healing. Keep walking. Grace is carrying you.

God Doesn't Waste Pain

Pain is one of life's most universal experiences. Whether it comes through loss, betrayal, disappointment, or hardship, pain touches every heart at some point. But as believers, we hold onto a profound truth—**God doesn't waste pain.**

God is not indifferent to your suffering. He is not a distant observer unmoved by your tears. Psalm 56:8 reminds us that God keeps track of every tear you shed; He collects them in a bottle, and records them in His book. That means not one moment of anguish escapes His attention. He sees. He knows. And He cares.

Romans 8:28 gives us a foundational promise: *"And we know that in all things God works for the good of those who love Him, who have been called according to His purpose."* Notice that it doesn't say all things are good—it says God works in *all things* for good. Even in your pain, even in your confusion, even in your darkest night, God is at work.

Every tear you've cried, every season you thought would break you, every valley you walked through in silence—**none of it is wasted.** God uses your wounds to refine your character, deepen your faith, strip away false securities, and draw you closer to Him. Pain is often the soil where perseverance, humility, and spiritual maturity grow.

Sometimes what feels like a delay or a detour is actually divine direction. You may think you're off course because of the pain, but in God's economy, pain is often the very path to your destiny. It shapes you for the assignment He has prepared for you. It tenderizes your heart for compassion, equips you with experience, and empowers your testimony.

Joseph's story in Genesis is a powerful example. Sold into slavery by his own brothers, wrongfully accused, and thrown into prison—yet, through every painful step, God was positioning him for purpose. At the end of his journey, Joseph declared to his brothers, *"You meant evil against me, but God meant it for good"* (Genesis 50:20). That same truth applies to your life.

So don't despise your pain. Bring it to God. Lay it at His feet. Let Him transform it. He is the Master Potter, and even your broken pieces are valuable in His hands. Your scars can become stories of healing. Your trials can birth testimonies. And your suffering can become a stage for His glory.

In the hands of God, **pain becomes purpose.** So hold on. Trust Him. You are not forsaken. You are being formed.

You're Not Alone—Others Are Bleeding Too
One of the enemy's most effective strategies is isolation. When you're hurting, he whispers lies that no one else feels what you feel, that your struggle is unique in its depth, that your pain is somehow shameful or abnormal. But the truth is this: **you are not alone.** Pain is part of the human experience, and though each story is different, the ache is familiar to many.

All around you, people are quietly bleeding—behind polished appearances, behind strong fronts, behind social media smiles. Some wear their wounds visibly, asking for help. Others mask their pain in silence, afraid of judgment, afraid of rejection, or simply weary from trying to explain. But know this: there are countless others walking through dark valleys—just like you. You're not weak because you're struggling; you're human.

Community is not a luxury—it's a lifeline. The body of Christ was never meant to suffer in silence. We were created to carry one another's burdens (Galatians 6:2), to lift each other up when we fall, to be a refuge for one another when the storms rage.

Don't isolate yourself. Don't believe the lie that no one would understand. **Reach out.** Share your story, even if your voice trembles. Allow yourself to be seen, known, and loved in the midst of your mess. And equally important—**listen.** When we gather in vulnerability and authenticity, something powerful happens: *healing multiplies.*

God doesn't waste pain. He redeems it. The comfort you've received during your lowest moments becomes the very balm you offer to others when they are hurting. As Scripture reminds us:

"Praise be to the God and Father of our Lord Jesus Christ, the Father of compassion and the God of all comfort, who comforts us in all our troubles, so that we can comfort those in any trouble with the comfort we ourselves receive from God."—2 Corinthians 1:3-4 (NIV)

So, if you're bleeding right now—emotionally, spiritually, mentally—know that there is hope. There is healing. And there is a family in Christ waiting to walk with you through it. Let your vulnerability become a doorway for connection and let your pain become a vessel for compassion.

You are not alone. And you never have to be. **Your greatest ministry may come from your deepest wound.**

Some of the most impactful ministries and testimonies are not birthed in comfort or ease, but in the furnace of affliction. Pain has a mysterious way of becoming the soil in which purpose grows. Your suffering is not wasted. In God's hands, your deepest wounds can become your most powerful witness. That heartbreak that shattered your soul, that betrayal that left you questioning your worth, that loss that silenced your joy—none of it is in vain.

The very area where you have bled the most may become the place where God uses you to bring healing to others. That season where you felt unloved may qualify you to speak life into someone who feels invisible. That moment when grief drowned your hope may prepare you to comfort others walking through the shadows. Your scars may not disappear, but they can serve as living proof that wounds can heal and that God is a Restorer.

Don't hide your story. Don't be ashamed of where you've been or what you've gone through. Your mess may become your message. Your trial may become someone else's lifeline. Your story may be the answer to someone's desperate prayer. The enemy wanted to use your pain to destroy you, but God can use it to develop you — and then deploy you.

Let God use your story. He is the only One who can turn a breakdown into a breakthrough, wounds into weapons for good, and pain into a platform for purpose. In His hands, scars don't mean you're damaged—they mean you survived. They mean grace showed up. They mean hope is real.

Your bleeding is not the end—it's the beginning of something beautiful. You are still here for a reason. Every breath you take is evidence that God is not finished with you yet. Keep pressing into Him. When the pain feels pointless, trust that heaven is still writing. When you feel forgotten, remember that God is most present in the silence. When your path feels uncertain, know that He is guiding you—even if it's one trembling step at a time.

Don't rush the process. Healing takes time. Ministry takes shape slowly. But as you heal, as you grow, as you rise again—others will watch and find strength to do the same. Your life will shout of a God who redeems. A God who restores. A God who never wastes pain.

So, lift your head. You're not just surviving—you're being prepared. Your story isn't over yet, and when it's fully written, it will testify of a God who brings **beauty from bleeding, strength from suffering, and miracles from messes.**

Let your wound become a wellspring of healing. Let your story bring light to someone else's darkness. Because sometimes, your greatest ministry doesn't begin on a platform—but in the pit. And from that pit, God raises deliverers.

APPENDICES

1. Reflection Questions After Each Chapter

These questions are designed to help the reader internalize and apply the truths discussed in each chapter. They serve as personal prompts for deep introspection, spiritual realignment, and practical next steps. Use them individually for journaling or collectively in group discussions.

Examples:
- *What part of this chapter resonated most deeply with your current season of leadership?*
- *In what ways have you been ministering while bleeding, and how has that affected your spiritual health?*
- *What boundaries need to be re-established to protect your soul and your calling?*
- *What would healing look like for you practically and spiritually in this area?*

2. Prayers for Wounded Leaders

These heartfelt prayers are crafted for leaders who have been bruised by betrayal, exhaustion, moral failure, or ministry disappointment. Whether whispered in solitude or read aloud in desperation, they offer words when you've lost your own.

Sample Titles:
- *A Prayer for the Betrayed Heart*
- *A Prayer for Burnt-Out Hands*
- *A Prayer for the Silent Wound*
- *A Prayer for the Restoration of Vision*

- *A Prayer to Minister Again Without Fear*

3. Scriptures for Comfort and Restoration
God's Word remains a healing balm for broken hearts. This section compiles specific verses of comfort, strength, and restoration that wounded leaders can cling to in moments of despair, guilt, or deep discouragement.

Examples:

- *Isaiah 40:29–31* – Strength for the weary.
- *Psalm 34:18* – The Lord is close to the brokenhearted.
- *Jeremiah 30:17* – "I will restore health to you..."
- *2 Corinthians 4:8–9* – Hard-pressed but not crushed.
- *Romans 8:1* – No condemnation for those in Christ.

This is a toolkit of truth—a scriptural anchor for stormy days.

4. Mental Health and Ministry Resources
Leadership doesn't require ignoring emotional pain. This section provides recommended resources—books, websites, Christian counseling networks, hotlines, and podcasts—that address the intersection of mental health and spiritual leadership.

Examples Include:
- Christian therapy networks (e.g., *Faithful Counseling, Focus on the Family's Counseling Services*)
- Burnout prevention resources and checklists.
- Books like *"Emotionally Healthy Leader"* by Peter Scazzero or *"Leading on Empty"* by Wayne Cordeiro.
- Mental health podcasts by Christian professionals.
- Sabbath and retreat center directories for spiritual renewal.

Note: Seeking help is not a weakness; it is wisdom. Healing starts with permission to be human again.

5. Testimonials from Other Leaders Who Have Bled

You are not alone. Many leaders have walked through the valleys of betrayal, moral failure, emotional collapse, and near-shipwreck—and found hope on the other side. These stories are shared anonymously or with permission, offering solidarity and a reminder: your pain has a purpose, and your story is not over.

Themes Include:
- *"I Nearly Quit the Ministry—But God Met Me in My Cave."*
- *"Restoration After Moral Failure: A Journey Back to the Altar."*
- *"From Bitterness to Forgiveness: Healing from Church Hurt."*
- *"How Sabbatical Saved My Family and My Ministry."*

These are not just stories—they are proof that God still restores the broken and rebuilds the fallen.

www.ingramcontent.com/pod-product-compliance
Lightning Source LLC
Chambersburg PA
CBHW051922160426
43198CB00012B/1994